Theodosia Burr

TEEN EYEWITNESS TO THE
FOUNDING OF THE NEW NATION

Karen Cherro Quiñones

TWENTY-FIRST CENTURY BOOKS / MINNEAPOLIS

This book is for my parents, who encouraged their unique daughter to pursue her talents, wherever they lead. And to loving fathers everywhere who support and strengthen their daughters.

Acknowledgments

Much of the research for this book was through original materials from historical societies and libraries in New York City, especially the New York Public Library (NYPL) Research Division and the New-York Historical Society. Infoweb's Newsbank database (a subscription service offered at NYPL) provided access to historical newspapers. The written biographies of Aaron Burr and Theodosia Burr are part of my personal collection. Some of the sources are also available online.

There is nothing better than period publications to help imagine what the past was like. The Vanderlyn portraits of Aaron and Theodosia Burr in the New-York Historical Society main gallery are mesmerizing and bring father and daughter to life. We are fortunate in New York City to have such a cast collection of historic documents, prints, and portraits available to us. I could not have done this book without the work of previous Burr biographers such as Matthew L. Davis, who carefully collected and organized Aaron Burr's personal and professional correspondence. And thank you to libraries around the world that have made their books available on the Internet Archive for everyone to find.

Twenty-First Century Books™
An imprint of Lerner Publishing Group, Inc.
241 First Avenue North
Minneapolis, MN 55401 USA

For reading levels and more information, look up this title at www.lernerbooks.com.

Main body text set in Adobe Garamond Pro.
Typeface provided by Adobe Systems.

Library of Congress Cataloging-in-Publication Data

Names: Quiñones, Karen Cherro, 1960– author.
Title: Theodosia Burr : teen eyewitness to the founding of the new nation / by Karen Cherro Quiñones.
Other titles: Teen eyewitness to the founding of the new nation
Description: Minneapolis : Twenty-First Century Books, [2020] | Includes bibliographical references and
    index. |
Identifiers: LCCN 2019009209 (print) | LCCN 2019010690 (ebook) | ISBN 9781541581753 (eb pdf) |
    ISBN 9781541542754 (library bound : alk. paper)
Subjects: LCSH: Alston, Theodosia Burr, 1783–1813. | Burr, Aaron, 1756–1836—Family. | Burr family.
    | United States—Politics and government—1783–1865. | New York (N.Y)—Social life and
    customs—18th century. | Alston, Joseph, 1778–1816—Family. | Socialites—New York (State)—
    New York—Biography. | Gifted women—United States—Biography. | Teenage girls—United
    States—Biography.
Classification: LCC E302.6.B9 (ebook) | LCC E302.6.B9 Q85 2020 (print) | DDC 973.4/6092 [B]—
    dc23

LC record available at https://lccn.loc.gov/2019009209

Manufactured in the United States of America
1-45422-39659-8/1/2019

Contents

Author's Note

Historians and biographers have written hundreds of books about the founding period of the United States of America and the people who participated. George Washington, John Adams, James Madison, Thomas Jefferson, Alexander Hamilton, and Aaron Burr are household names in the twenty-first century. While studying my home city, New York, and the events that occurred here, I became interested in the everyday life of that exciting time. What was it like to witness President Washington's inauguration in 1789, to walk down the street and see the founding fathers and their families going about everyday tasks? Searching through firsthand accounts to learn more, I discovered the story of Theodosia Burr, Aaron Burr's daughter.

Theodosia grew up in New York City at the same time the nation was growing up. She met many of the people who had a role in shaping the future of the city and the country. Like the new nation, she too was an experiment. The United States was an experiment in government elected by the people. Theodosia Burr was the first woman of her time to be educated in the same way that men were. Her parents believed women would have a new role in the United States, a role that required accomplished, capable individuals. And they set out to prove it with their daughter.

Most of what we know about Theodosia Burr is through letters. For most of her young life, her father was away serving in the new US government. The earliest accounts of her are in letters between her mother and father and, eventually, between Theodosia and her father. It is through these missives that we can put together the story of an unusual girl, growing up in a rigidly structured social class while, at the same time, pursuing a radical, new path for girls and women.

Theodosia Burr didn't publish a book or leave anything behind other than family letters. However, we can find observations of her in memoirs written by people who knew her. Those memoirs and the correspondence between Theodosia Burr and her father as well as between her parents are all available in New York City in various library collections. The New York Public Library's Rare Books and Manuscripts Divisions and the New-York Historical Society have transferred most of this material to digital format, where it is easily accessible on-site. Visitors can request and view by appointment the unconverted items. Viewing an actual letter written by nine-year-old Theodosia in 1791 was indescribably exciting for me.

I've studied these resources and used them to bring Theodosia Burr to life. Who were her friends, and what was her daily life? What was it like to be a teenaged girl when strict expectations limited what a young woman could aspire to? And what was it like to be raised with beliefs that were contrary to those expectations? I've tried to open a window into her life and times through which we can all peer.

This is also the story of dedicated parents and, especially, a devoted and sometimes overbearing father. Aaron Burr is remembered as a notorious figure in American history, but privately, he was a loving, attentive husband and father. Burr poured everything into his gifted daughter, offering her the privileges and advantages a son would have had. He shaped her into his own image of a type of woman who did not exist at the time. As a father, Burr never doubted that his daughter could attain the highest levels of scholarly success. He was not disappointed.

1

A New Nation

The whole city was one scene of triumphal rejoicing. His name in every form of decoration appeared on the fronts of the houses.

—Eliza Morton, fifteen, eyewitness to George Washington's inauguration, diary entry, 1821

When George Washington was president, 225 years ago, a girl different from all others was growing up in New York City. She was well educated, even though girls were not allowed to go to school. By the time she was in her teens, she was fluent in French and could read and write Latin and Greek. While her father was away from home serving as a US senator, she held a formal state dinner for some of the most important people in New York, impressing them all. As a young woman, she was taught by the most excellent teachers available. Her name was Theodosia Burr. This is her story.

CHEERING FOR THE PRESIDENT

Thousands of people filled the intersection of Wall and Broad Streets on April 30, 1789. Excitement and expectation flowed through the cheering crowd on this late spring day. They had come to New York City from the northern parts of Maine and southernmost Georgia and

George Washington delivered his inaugural address in New York City's Federal Hall on April 30, 1789. In the mid-nineteenth century, American artist Tompkins Harrison Matteson painted an image of the event, from which British artist Henry S. Sadd made this engraving.

from as far away as France to celebrate the inauguration of the first president of the United States, George Washington. Observers leaned out of the windows of nearby buildings to get a good view. The crowd swelled westward up Broadway, southward down Broad Street, and eastward to William Street. All rooms in or near the city were full.

At last, George Washington, wearing a brown suit, appeared on the second-floor balcony of the Federal Hall. Washington and his vice president, John Adams, wore American-made rather than European clothing, to demonstrate the nation's ability to compete with the best the world had to offer.

Dressed in black judicial robes, Chancellor Robert Livingston, the highest-ranking judicial official in New York, recited the presidential oath for the first time. Washington, his hand on a Bible held by Samuel Allyne Otis, secretary of the Senate, repeated after Livingston, "I do solemnly swear (or affirm) that I will faithfully execute the Office of President of the United States, and will to the best of my Ability, preserve, protect and

A New Nation

defend the Constitution of the United States." Washington added, "So help me God." At that moment, a new country with a constitution to guide its leaders came fully into being. It would be a nation of laws, ruled by the people themselves, not by a king or a queen. The United States of America would offer opportunities to its people that had never existed before.

The crowd erupted into wild applause and shouts of approval. Five-year-old Theodosia Burr was in the crowd with her father, New York's young prominent attorney general Aaron Burr, and his wife, Theodosia. The Burrs were already busy planning an unprecedented future for their daughter. But on that day, for a few hours, she was just another five-year-old girl cheering for Washington.

BEGINNINGS

Theodosia Burr was born on June 21, 1783, at the Burr home in Albany, New York. She was named after her maternal grandfather, Theodosius Bartow. The name Theodosius comes from the ancient Greek language and means "gift of God." It was customary at that time for parents to name their children after their own parents. In Theodosia's case, her name was also her mother's first name.

Her thirty-six-year-old mother had suffered two miscarriages before this. She and her husband, twenty-six-year-old Aaron Burr, and her children from a previous marriage were elated at the arrival of a healthy baby girl. Aaron Burr opened his best bottle of Madeira wine to celebrate and invited the neighbors to join them.

Later that day, he sat down and wrote birth announcements to his friends. In his excitement, he used his formal business signature rather than the more casual personal signature that

> "No daughter ever received a heartier welcome to the home and hearts of her parents, and none ever awakened a greater parental care and solicitude than did she."
>
> —Charles Burr Todd, Aaron Burr biographer, 1879

Federal Hall

"The windows and roofs of the houses were crowded; and in the streets the throng was so dense, that it seemed as if one might literally walk on the heads of the people."

—Eliza Morton, fifteen, eyewitness to George Washington's inauguration, diary entry, 1821

The first Congress of the United States unanimously elected George Washington in 1789 as the nation's first president. John Adams won the second highest number of votes from Congress to become Washington's vice president.

Washington was inaugurated on April 30, 1789, on the balcony of Federal Hall in New York City. Federal Hall stood at the intersection of Wall and Broad Streets. Architect Pierre L'Enfant, a former French officer in the American Revolution, had supervised the renovation of the old New York City Hall for the inauguration. Before then the building had been the centerpiece of New York's colonial government and had hosted meetings of the colonial assembly. In 1735 the trial of printer John Peter Zenger, which established the free press in the colony of New York, was held there. In 1765 the Stamp Act Congress, the first congress of the American colonies, had met inside the building to organize the colonies in opposition to the Stamp Act.

In 1842, about fifty years after Washington's inauguration, the building was replaced with a customs house. The designers created the building to look like a blend of the famous columns of the Parthenon in Athens, Greece, and the dome of the Pantheon in Rome, Italy.

This hand-colored photograph of an engraving from the late eighteenth century shows Federal Hall in New York with a group of people on the balcony, where George Washington was inaugurated in 1789.

In the twenty-first century, the building is a national monument—Federal Hall National Memorial—and is owned by the US National Park Service. Learn more about the building and its history at www.nps.gov/feha/index.htm.

New York painter John Vanderlyn created this portrait of Aaron Burr in 1802. Burr supported the young artist for many years, providing financial support for him to study abroad and to paint.

letter-writing etiquette would have called for. His wife later apologized to their friends for the error, explaining that her husband had been overcome with emotion.

The Burr household filled with happiness that summer. Aaron Burr had recently passed the New York bar exam, allowing him to practice law legally in New York, and he was beginning his legal career. The American Revolution (1775–1783) was over, and the final peace treaty with England was about to be signed in Paris, France. The Burrs, like other American patriots who supported freedom from British rule, were eagerly looking forward to life in a new and independent United States of America.

Aaron Burr and his wife, the former Theodosia Prévost, had their sights set on something almost as significant: moving to and helping establish New York City on the island of Manhattan as a center of commerce and government. Their plans temporarily stalled while they waited for the departure of British troops, which had occupied the city since 1776. Albany, where the Burrs lived when Theodosia was born, was the second-biggest city in New York and lay about 150 miles (240 km) to the north of New York City on the magnificent Hudson River. During the war, Albany had been the temporary home for many patriot families who had fled the city for safety. With peace, the migration southward back to the island of Manhattan would begin.

The Lenape

The Lenape people of North America were also called Leni Lenape, Lenni Lenape, or Delaware (a European name for the Lenape). Their territory spanned part of the Hudson River valley of New York State, western Long Island, eastern Pennsylvania, New Jersey, and Delaware. The Lenape spoke similar languages and shared family ties.

In the seventeenth century, the Lenape trapped beaver and traded beaver pelts with Dutch settlers for European goods. Their population declined significantly from exposure to infectious European diseases such as smallpox and measles as well as through warfare with Europeans and the indigenous peoples of Upstate New York. Some of the surviving Lenape lived within the colony and city of New York, attempting to blend in with the growing population there. Others were forced westward into Pennsylvania and beyond. These days, small numbers of Lenape live in Oklahoma, Wisconsin, and in the Canadian province of Ontario.

THE ISLAND AT THE CENTER OF THE WORLD

New York City has existed on the island of Manhattan since the seventeenth century. The indigenous Lenape people, who had lived there for thousands of years, called the island Mannahatta. In 1609 the English explorer Henry Hudson sailed into the large, deep-water harbor at the tip of the island and from there northward along the western shore of Mannahatta. Overwhelmed, he sent reports back to England of the region's natural beauty, abundance of beaver, and the friendliness of the Lenape. After that, more European expeditions came to the area. English and Dutch fur traders settled along the river on what was later called Long Island (to the east of Manhattan) and in what eventually became northern New Jersey. European traders collected beaver pelts from indigenous trappers in exchange for food crops and other European goods. Furriers processed the pelts so they could be made into leather for hats, and then they shipped the pelts down the Hudson to the Atlantic Ocean. From there they went to European markets, where the pelts sold for top prices.

The fur trade led the way for European colonization of the North American continent. In 1626 Peter Minuit, acting for the Dutch West India Company, bought most of what later became the state of New York from the Lenape. The Dutch called their colony New Netherland and established a village, New Amsterdam, on the southern tip of Manhattan. The Dutch and Lenape lived peacefully until the arrival of Dutch governor William

Originally drawn in 1660 by the surveyor Jacques Cortelyou, this map of New Amsterdam was lost and then rediscovered in 1900 at the Villa di Castello near Florence, Italy. So the map is known as the Castello Plan.

The New York City Flag and Seal

The New York City flag and seal (*right*) depict the city's history of colonization. The colors—blue, white, and orange—represent the colors of the Dutch flag when the city was part of the Dutch colony of New Netherland. In the center of the seal is a Dutch windmill. On the top and bottom of the windmill are beavers, symbolizing the fur trade. Barrels on the sides of the windmill represent commerce. To the right of the windmill is a Lenape man, and to the left is a Dutch sailor. The year 1625, at the base of the windmill, is the year the Dutch established New Netherland. The seal is crowned with a bald eagle—a symbol of the United States. The legend *Sigillum Civitatis Novi Eboraci* is Latin for "the Seal of the City of New York."

Kieft in 1638. In 1643, without the support of the people of New Amsterdam, he ordered a brutal attack on the Lenape people in which 120 innocent Lenape, including women and children, were murdered by Dutch soldiers. This lead to what is today known as Kieft's War. The raid prompted surrounding tribes to join forces, and for three years the united tribes fought with settlers along the Hudson Valley. Both sides suffered losses. The people of New Netherland had Kieft removed from his position and sent back to the Netherlands. This resulted in a renewed peace between the Lenape and Dutch.

By the 1660s, the settlement was thriving on trade, and New Amsterdam had become a bustling maritime village of twenty-five hundred people, about one-third of the colony's nine thousand inhabitants. For protection from the threat of an English invasion, the Dutch built a wall along the village's northern border, where Wall Street is.

Meanwhile, England was building colonies to the north and south of Manhattan. England's "twelve trans-Atlantic daughters" (American colonies) had a "stranger within her gates" (the Dutch in Manhattan). England set out to take control by invading New Amsterdam in 1664. The Dutch had no colonial army, so the people of New Amsterdam persuaded the Dutch governor, Peter Stuyvesant, to surrender. Neither side fired a shot. The colony became New York under British control.

In 1669 the British tore down the northern border wall and the village expanded northward to what later became Chambers Street. By the time the first shots of the American Revolution were fired at Lexington and Concord in Massachusetts in 1775, New York City had grown to twenty-five thousand people crowded into less than 1 square mile (2.6 sq. km). People came from every direction to enjoy the opportunities the port town offered. Strolling along the Broad Way through the center of town on a busy afternoon, it was common to hear English, Dutch, Spanish, German, French, and a bit of Italian and Arabic. The steeple of Trinity Church stood as a reminder that the Church of England was the official government religion. The city also had houses of worship for Jews, Quakers, Lutherans, Methodists, Moravians, Presbyterians, and Dutch Reformed.

The colony of New York had some of the most liberal voting rights in North America. If a man owned property, was a master tradesman, or met other qualifications, he was able to vote regardless of his race or religion. Women could not vote but often helped run family businesses. Daughters of successful families in the Netherlands started some of New York's original Dutch companies. Many of their daughters and granddaughters continued to manage those businesses under British colonial law, which denied women the right to own property or businesses. The women of New York successfully exerted their influence in business and politics from behind the scenes.

REVOLUTION COMES TO NEW YORK

The Knickerbockers, as popular American author Washington Irving called New Yorkers, lived together peacefully. They went about their daily routines of work, school, shopping, and socializing. But when Israel Bissell arrived on April 23, 1775, and announced to a crowd on the commons, a public park, that American men had been killed by British troops at Lexington and Concord, the town descended into chaos. New Yorkers divided into patriots and Loyalists (people who were loyal to British rule in the American colonies). Neighbors became rivals, and families split along political lines. The following year, the American Revolution came to New York.

George Washington's army arrived in early 1776 to defend the island against the coming British invasion. People fled the island in fear. Most went to stay with relatives or friends in New Jersey or on Long Island, expecting to return after the battle was over.

The war brought difficult times to the city. A massive fire destroyed a quarter of the town in September 1776. British forces had established the city as a military base. Homes became barracks, and storehouses became jails for prisoners of war. The magnificent steeple of Trinity Church was gone, destroyed in the fire of 1776. One neighborhood, filled with the ruins of homes destroyed in the fire, became a canvas town. There, inhabitants put up canvas tarps to cover the missing roofs. Martial law, or military control, replaced civilian rule.

At last, in 1783, representatives of the United States and Great Britain signed the Treaty of Paris, ending the war. British soldiers went home. New Yorkers who had lived in exile returned and set about to rebuild, grow, and prosper. Their determination paid off when New York was chosen in 1785 to be the nation's first capital city.

2
The Colonel and the Widow

Theodosia [Prévost] first made him [Aaron Burr] respect the intellect of women, and to [her] he owed the happiest hours and happiest years of existence.

—James Parton, Aaron Burr biographer

Theodosia Burr's father, Aaron Burr, was born on February 6, 1756, in New Jersey. His maternal grandfather was Jonathan Edwards, a well-known intellectual and theologian, or religious scholar. Aaron's father, the Reverend Aaron Burr Sr., was one of his students. Burr Sr. was a graduate of Yale College. He married Edwards's daughter Esther Edwards. They settled near Princeton, New Jersey, where Burr started a college, the College of New Jersey, in 1746. The school was renamed Princeton in 1756 for the town nearby and later became Princeton University.

Aaron and his older sister, Sarah, became young orphans when their father died in 1757 and their mother, in 1758, from an unrecorded illness. Their uncle Timothy Edwards eventually took them in and raised them in his home in Elizabeth, New Jersey. Aaron was a child prodigy, excelling at English, history, Latin, and Greek.

This illustration of Princeton appeared in a 1764 guide to the college. It shows the main school, Nassau Hall (*left*), and the college president's house (*right*). Aaron Burr's father founded the school in 1746.

He applied to Princeton when he was only eleven years old. He passed the entrance exam, but the college did not accept him because he was so young. Aaron continued his studies, and when he was thirteen, the college admitted him to the sophomore class even though he qualified academically for the junior class. He received a bachelor of arts degree when he was sixteen years old.

Unsure of a profession, Aaron stayed at Princeton to continue his liberal arts studies. In 1773, when he was seventeen, he moved to Bethlehem, Connecticut, where he studied theology with Joseph Bellamy, who had studied under Burr's grandfather, Jonathan Edwards. The following summer, Burr moved to Litchfield, Connecticut, where his sister, now married, lived. Burr began to study law with his sister's husband, lawyer Tapping Reeve. When he learned about the battles of Lexington and Concord in 1775, Burr enlisted in the Continental Army (the army of the American colonies) and received a captain's commission.

College in the 1770s

In the eighteenth century, the most popular and prestigious colleges in and around New York City were Yale College in Connecticut, Princeton College in New Jersey, and Columbia (formerly King's College) in New York City. They all are still highly ranked universities.

Then only boys attended college. They took college admission exams when they were fourteen or fifteen years old and were required to have some knowledge of English history, Greek and Roman history and mythology, philosophy, math, and European literature. As part of the application, the student was required to translate both a Latin and a Greek document into English. Yale and Princeton also required a translation of a Hebrew document into English.

Boys began preparing for college when they were five years old by learning to read and write. At ten they started to learn Latin and Greek. By fourteen they had acquired a good knowledge of other required subjects for entrance into college. American society did not think girls were capable of this kind of learning, so they received minimal education at home.

After college, young men apprenticed with, or learned skills from, a professional in their chosen career until they were ready to go out on their own. Some professions, such as the law, required that a person pass the state bar exam to be formally admitted to the field.

This undated illustration shows King's College (which eventually became Columbia University) in New York City as it looked in 1756.

By 1778 Burr had become Colonel Burr, commanding a regiment based in New Jersey. About 16 miles (26 km) from his camp, in the town of Paramus, the Prévost family lived. Colonel Jacques-Marc Prévost (of Genevese ancestry) was a major in the British army. He was fighting in the Caribbean islands. (Because of the strategic location of the islands, the British and the Americans fought for control of this region during the American Revolution.) While Prévost was away, his wife, Theodosia Bartow Prévost, ran their home, the Hermitage. She raised their two sons, John Bartow and Augustine Frederick, and three daughters, Sally, Anna Louisa, and Mary Louisa. Her mother, Ann De Visme, and her half sister, known only as Miss De Visme, were part of the household. Historian James Parton described them this way, saying, "The ladies were accomplished and intelligent; for a long time their house had been the center of the elegant society of the vicinity, and after the Revolution had begun, officers of rank in the American army still visited them." Burr was among those officers.

Burr and Theodosia Prévost were instantly attracted to each other. Burr became a regular visitor to the Hermitage, where he and

Invisible Women

Historians have extensive information about Theodosia Prévost's sons, including the dates of their births, education, professional lives, marriages, and children. Yet they know little about the females in her life, including her sister, known only in documents as Miss de Visme. There is also some discrepancy about whether Theodosia Prévost had two or three daughters. At that time, women and their lives were not valued in the same way as men and their lives. Information about women's lives was rarely recorded. So when modern historians do historic research, it is often difficult to find specific information about women in earlier centuries. The lack of sources is frustrating and presents an obstacle to forming a good understanding of women's lives, the role they played as events unfolded, and their thoughts about and influence on those events.

Theodosia Prévost discussed politics, philosophy, theology, and science. Burr, who was ten years younger than she was, often stayed long into the night, rushing back to rejoin his regiment before morning. His fellow officers teased him about his attraction to the married woman, who was described as an attractive, though not beautiful, woman. A mother of five with a scar on her forehead, society considered her past her prime years of beauty. Her elegant manners, intellect, and the respect she received from all who met her were irresistible to Burr.

The two were both fluent in French, an important world language that most educated Americans learned. French was an international language, used in diplomacy and in social gatherings with people from different countries. The couple was able to communicate easily with each other in French. They read books by French philosopher Jean-Jacques Rousseau and French playwright Voltaire, which the Prévost family had in the collection of the Hermitage library. The two discussed their readings, and Burr was entranced by her intellect, which he found to be equal to his own. He couldn't stay away. Gossip spread about the scandalous amount of time Burr was spending at the Prévost home, but his upstanding character protected them from the rumors. She wrote to him about the rumors, saying, "Our being the subject of much inquiry, conjecture, and calumny [harmful, false statements], was no more than we ought to expect. My attention to you was ever pointed enough to attract the observation of those who visited the house. Your esteem more than compensated for the worst they could say."

Burr was hooked. This kind of woman had existed up to this point only in his imagination, a woman no one at the time believed could exist—an intellectual. In the United States of the late eighteenth century, women, even those in the wealthiest families, were minimally educated outside of the domestic skills they would need as wives and mothers. Instead, they were taught skills from childhood that were deemed more important for women to know. For upper-class girls like Theodosia that would include embroidery, drawing, painting, flower arranging, etiquette, and social planning. Other girls would learn to cook, clean, sew, do farm chores, and other tasks needed to keep the household running in good order. The nation's Founding Fathers chose their wives for their potential as nurturing mothers, educators for the children that would eventually come, and as social ornaments.

Reading and writing were considered necessary for women only for general use such as writing letters and teaching children to read and write. Theodosia Prévost, however, was educated in philosophy, Greek and Roman classical literature, and read and wrote French fluently. She possessed a sharp mind and quick wit, as did he, and was able to keep up with his fast thinking. Burr valued this in her more than her appearance, wealth, or status. Historian Henry Bischoff says of Theodosia Prévost, "Her knowledge of languages, her analytic abilities and her habits of reading indicate an education at home that was far above that received by most privileged women in the colonial New York/New Jersey area." As for Theodosia Prévost, she found that Burr appreciated the qualities in her that so many others considered strange in a woman. Theirs was a new kind of relationship between a man and a woman—an alliance of equals.

Colonel Prévost was killed in action in 1779. Mail went by boat and was extremely slow, so word of his death didn't get to the family in New Jersey until 1781. This news cleared the way for them to marry. On July 2, 1782, three months after Burr gained admission to the New York Bar Association, they were married at the Hermitage.

Years later, Burr wrote to his wife about how much she had changed him and his thinking about women: "It was the knowledge of your mind which first inspired me with a respect for that of your sex, and with some regret, I confess, that the ideas which you have often heard me express in favour of female intellectual powers are founded on what I have imagined, more than what I have seen except in you. I have endeavored to trace the causes of this rare display of genius in women and find them in the errors of education, of prejudice, of habit."

The Hermitage

Theodosia Burr grew up in Ho-Ho-Kus, New Jersey. She lived in a home, eventually known as the Hermitage (*below*), which her mother's first husband had bought in 1767. In 1782 Aaron Burr and Theodosia Prévost were married there. In 1847 the house was remodeled in the Gothic Revival style, with steep, pointed roofs; scrollwork; and diamond-shaped windowpanes. Various families owned it over the years, and it eventually became a national and New Jersey historic landmark. The home is open to the public as a museum. Learn more at the Hermitage website at http://thehermitage.org/.

After the wedding, the Burrs, including her children Frederick (sixteen), John Bartow (fourteen), Anna Lousia, Mary Louisa, and Sally (ages not known) moved to Albany to live as a family. (Historians are not sure of the ages of the Prévost daughters, as the custom of the time was to record only the birth dates of the boys.) Burr was a generous man who loved and cared for the children as if they were his own. They, in turn, called him Papa, loving him and looking up to him as a father.

Burr's friend and biographer, Matthew Davis, recalled, "In the education of Mrs. Burr's children by her first husband he took a deep interest. Neither labour or expense was regarded. It was his wish that they should be accomplished, well educated men." Frederick and John went on to work as clerks in Burr's law practice. Frederick eventually became a farmer. John became a lawyer and a superior court judge in Louisiana.

3
On to New York City

Your dear little Theo grows the most engaging child you ever saw.
—*Theodosia Prévost Burr, in a letter to Aaron Burr, 1785*

Theodosia was born in the family's temporary home in Albany, New York, during the final year of the revolution, while Americans awaited a final peace treaty with England. The following year, the family relocated to New York City. As the rosy-cheeked Miss Priss (an affectionate term Theodosia's mother used for her) took her first steps in the small, wood-framed Burr home on Maiden Lane, the city of New York was taking giant steps into its future as the nation's premier city. New Yorkers, free of external rule for the first time, pondered their future.

Newspapers and pamphlets presented ideas and counter ideas. New Yorkers discussed the pressing issues with their neighbors and friends. In the midst of the postwar commotion, Burr opened a law practice in the city. A few blocks away lived another young lawyer, Alexander Hamilton. He too had come to the city from Albany, with his wife, Eliza, and their baby son, Philip.

Burr quickly became a well-respected lawyer, and in 1784, he was elected to the New York Assembly. He served two sessions, in 1784

In 1795, when Theodosia was eleven, American artist Gilbert Stuart painted the first portrait of her. Stuart, one of the nation's most famous portraitists, had also painted her father the year before. Burr wrote to his daughter about the Stuart portrait of her, "Your picture is really quite like you; still it does not quite please me. It has a pensive, sentimental air; that of a love-sick maid!"

and 1785. Assembly sessions lasted only a few months. The lawmaking body met on Wall Street, just a few blocks away from the Burr home. This convenient location allowed him to spend much of his time at home to mentor his stepsons' education and nurture his little daughter. An adoring father, he showed off his beautiful baby girl to friends and associates.

During Burr's second term, lawmakers proposed a bill for the gradual abolition of slavery in New York. It required all slave owners to free any enslaved peoples born after the passage of the bill. Burr moved to change the proposed law to free all enslaved peoples and completely end slavery throughout the state of New York. His amendment failed, so Burr voted for the original bill. The Founding Fathers had not resolved whether the new nation would promote or abolish slavery. They left it to each state to decide its policies. Burr believed strongly that all people should be free and educated, regardless of sex or race. He and his wife followed those principals in the way they raised Theodosia.

During the years her father was in the assembly, Theodosia lived a normal childhood. She played with her friends and went out with her parents. She walked and talked and grew. Her health was a relief to her parents. This was a time before antibiotics and vaccinations, so measles, diphtheria, and many other childhood diseases could be fatal. The Burrs' second daughter, Sarah, died in 1788, when she was only three.

The Burrs had a full house, with children ranging in age from teenage Frederick to young Theodosia. Frederick and Theodosia were close, and their closeness continued throughout her life. When her father was traveling on business, her mother often wrote to him about the responsibilities at home and constant activity, which were, at times, overwhelming for her. She wrote to her husband of the fondness their daughter had for him. "She frequently talks of and calls on, her dear papa." The love between daughter and father would develop into a cherished closeness over the years, a closeness her mother observed, writing to Burr, "She was one whole day indifferent to everything but your name. Her attachment is not of a common nature."

After serving two terms in the assembly, Burr turned his full attention to his law practice. He eventually became one of the most in-demand and highest-paid lawyers in the city. Known for his expertise in New York State criminal and civil law and for his dedication to the preparation of each case, he built a large and prestigious practice. Barely thirty years old, he was highly respected. He was one of the city's young, bright, future stars.

"[Theodosia] has written to you and is anxious lest I should omit sending it. Toujours la vôtre, [always yours] Theodosia"

—Theodosia's mother to Aaron Burr, when their daughter was three years old, 1785

MUCH WORK TO BE DONE

Theodosia was five years old on the day in 1789 when she watched George Washington take the presidential oath of office a few blocks from her home. Everyone who was anyone was in New York that day, and many of them knew her parents. Washington had been her father's commander during the American Revolution. He and his wife, First Lady Martha Washington, knew her mother from visiting the Hermitage, where they would stop while traveling between battles. Burr's friends from Princeton were there too, including James Madison, part of the committee that wrote the nation's constitution, and his wife, Dolley Madison. (Burr had introduced the couple.) James Monroe, a friend of the Prévost family and like Madison a future president, was there too.

After the ratification of the US Constitution that year, New York's governor, George Clinton, nominated Burr to be the state's attorney general. As attorney general, Burr would serve as the main lawyer for the State of New York. The new nation's leaders knew they would be grappling with many difficult questions about the role of the federal government, as laid out in the Constitution, and that of the nation's state governments. What if a state law conflicted with the Constitution? The attorney general would figure out these issues and then argue the cases in court. Both Clinton and Burr belonged to the Anti-Federalist political party. They would work to limit federal control over states. Federalists believed in a strong central government. Federalist leaders at the time included John Adams, Alexander Hamilton, and John Jay.

One of the first issues Burr had to deal with involved legal ownership of property. When the British had occupied New York during the revolution, many people had fled their homes to live in surrounding areas. When they returned years later, after the war, they often found someone living on their property. That person or family might have been living there for as long as seven years (the

On to New York City

length of the war) and might have made improvements to the home and property. Disputes arose over who legally owned the land and whether the new residents owed rent to the original owners. Burr gained great respect for his fair and impartial handling of the cases that came before the court to decide ownership.

Burr's reputation and law practice grew, and so did his wife's involvement. A big part of Burr's success was his wife's brilliance, sound advice, and participation in his career. He once told a friend that she was his intellectual equal and moral superior and that he relied on her guidance in all matters. This was a stunning admission from a man of Burr's rank when most people believed women were incapable of moral judgment. Usually a man of his rank saw a wife as just a mother of his children and a social companion.

When Burr was away from the office traveling, his wife took over the law practice. She acted as the intermediary between Burr and his clients. She passed on to them all pertinent information concerning their legal cases and any communication from the clients back to her husband. Burr's clients came to depend on his wife as much as they did on him. "To him she was indeed a helpmate; for she not only had charge of his domestic concerns, but was counseled with, and intimately associated in, all his business transactions."

Little Theodosia spent her childhood in a busy, intellectually stimulating environment where her mother was as much a participant as her father. This was a very unusual home. The wives of men of Burr's status stayed at home, raised children, had afternoon tea, did needlework, and socialized with other women. The only time they might see their husband's legal clients would be at a social event and even then would have no understanding of the intricacies of a lawsuit.

As Theodosia observed the respect with which her father's peers regarded her mother, she learned that women were capable partners in life and business.

Compromise of 1790

When the American colonies fought for independence from Great Britain, they borrowed money from other countries to finance their government and military. The war decimated American towns, ports, and farms. Rebuilding would be expensive. But after the war was over, the new states struggled to repay their debts and to find the money to pay for rebuilding.

In 1790 Secretary of the Treasury Alexander Hamilton met with Virginia congressional representative James Madison and Secretary of State Thomas Jefferson at Jefferson's home on Maiden Lane in New York. They worked out a compromise that enabled the federal government to assume, or pay for, the debts of the states. In return, Virginia, which did not owe any money and therefore would not benefit from the deal, would be home to the nation's capital city. During the building of the new capital city in Virginia, the capital temporarily moved from New York City to Philadelphia, until 1801.

These portraits of famous early American leaders are (*from left to right*) Alexander Hamilton (by John Trumbull, 1806), Thomas Jefferson (by Gilbert Stuart, 1821), and James Madison (by John Vanderlyn, 1816).

AN EXCEPTIONAL LITTLE GIRL

In the eighteenth century, fathers carefully molded their firstborn sons so they would be prepared to take over their professions and surpass them in their success. The boys were expected to read and write by the time they were five years old and to begin studies in Latin and Greek at ten. Theodosia, at five, could read and write as well as the boys her age and speak some French. She had already written her first letters to her father. Theodosia learned alongside her older half sisters, who were also encouraged to achieve at reading, writing, and math.

In 1791, when Theodosia was eight years old, her father was elected to the US Senate and began to spend most of his time in Philadelphia. John Bartow accompanied him as his clerk. Frederick was married and lived on a farm in Pelham, north of Manhattan. So Theodosia, her half sisters, and her mother were constant companions, and her

Letter Writing

Writing letters was the main form of communication in the eighteenth century. Friends and family members often sent short notes to one another during the day, even if they lived only a few blocks away from one another. A servant or paid messenger would carry the notes back and forth.

The Burrs and other people separated by greater distances depended on the nation's new postal service, established as part of the ratification, or approval, of the US Constitution in 1789. During Theodosia's time, the nation had seventy-five post offices and about 2,000 miles (3,219 km) of postal roads. The Burrs often wrote to each other every day, even if the letters wouldn't arrive for a few days or a week or more. The letters Aaron Burr and his wife exchanged often crossed in the mail, with one asking a question while the other had already provided that information. Many families carefully preserved their written communications. In the twenty-first century, those letters serve as primary sources of information for historians, researchers, and writers.

mother became their teacher. Burr wrote to them daily and expected them to write back. Together, the Burrs attentively managed their gifted daughter's schooling. They even hired the same tutors for her that New Yorkers employed for their talented sons. These tutors were specialists in grammar, math, Latin, Greek, and geography.

> **"She writes and ciphers [does math] from five in the morning to eight and also the same hours in the evening."**
>
> —Theodosia's mother, when Theodosia was eight years old, 1791

In the summer of 1791, Theodosia's mother wrote to her husband about her concerns that their daughter's days were so crammed with activities that she was unable to focus well on any one subject. "Theo never can or will make the progress we would wish her while she has so many avocations [activities]," she said.

What was a day like for eight-year-old Theodosia? It began at five in the morning, with writing and math lessons that lasted until eight. During the day, she took French lessons, dancing lessons, and music lessons. Then, at five in the evening, she repeated her morning routine. Her mother wrote to her husband that Theodosia's progress in math surpassed her older half sister's efforts. "Theo makes amazing progress at figures. . . . You will really be surprised at her improvement. Though Louisa has worked at them all winter, yet Theo is now before her, and assists her to make her sums."

Theodosia also learned about personal appearance and social etiquette, and she was expected to master these subjects as well as her formal educational studies. Adults viewed children as miniature adults and dressed them in adult fashions. Theodosia's mother taught her daughter how to put on the many layers of petticoats, skirts, and blouses a lady's couture required at that time. She taught her to fix her hair and to walk and sit properly. Theodosia was instructed in the manners expected of her social class, such as how to greet people properly, respond to greetings and questions, and manage table manners for eating gracefully. As the daughter of a US senator and member of New York's upper class, she was expected to know the proper etiquette for all types of social interactions.

Busy with her studies, Theo often forgot to answer her father's letters or would start one and then become distracted. This annoyed Burr, who wrote repeatedly to her that she was neglecting her duties to him. Her mother defended her, responding to her husband, "Theo has begun to write several letters, but never finished one. The only time she has to write is also the hour of general leisure, and, when once she is interrupted, there is no making her return to work." Theodosia was, after all, a little girl, and like other little girls, she enjoyed playing with her dolls and her friends. Her mother gently reminded her husband that their daughter needed time to be a child.

> **"There is something on the style and arrangement of the words which would have done honor to a girl of sixteen."**
>
> —Aaron Burr, complimenting Theodosia's writing ability when she was nine, 1793

When Burr at last received a letter from his Little Miss Priss, he was elated. He wrote to her in return, saying, "Judge of my pleasure and surprise when I opened and found it was from my dear little girl. You improve much in your writing."

One of the earliest surviving letters from Theodosia was written when she was nine, to her half brother Frederick on his farm in Pelham. It demonstrates her early mastery of grammar and growing vocabulary. In it, she told her brother she had recovered from the mumps and hoped he was recovered as well. She reported that for dinner, she and her family had eaten the pig he had sent them. She told him that their papa had bought her an elegant fortepiano (a type of small piano).

Girls and Boys Clothes in the Late Eighteenth Century

From about the age of eight, girls were expected to dress like mini versions of proper ladies. From about that same age, boys dressed like mini versions of gentlemen. As an upper-class girl, Theodosia dressed every day in a laced-up corset, a silk gown worn over a petticoat, and stylish leather or silk shoes. Colorful ribbons tied in the hair or around the neck were also popular. In an informal setting, a girl would wear her hair loose under a broad-brimmed hat or with a bow. A boy would wear clothing like his father's, including leather shoes, leggings, breeches, a shirt, a vest, and a coat with a cravat (neckband), the forerunner of a modern necktie. In formal situations, such as a dance or dinner party, girls would wear formal dresses made of expensive fabrics reserved for special occasions. Boys would also wear higher-quality clothes set aside for such occasions.

John Durand painted this portrait of the Rapelje children in 1768. The Rapeljes were a wealthy merchant family in New York City. The children are, from left to right, Garret, George, Anne, and Jacques. They are dressed in typical fashions of the era, including ribbons in Anne's hair and around her neck and vests for the boys.

She decided against ending her letter with the traditional *affectionately,* saying with a little tease, "I am tired of affectionate, not of being it but of writing it, so I leave it out; I am your sister, Theodosia B. Burr."

THE KEYS TO SUCCESS

Frederick's sprawling farm at Pelham provided a relaxing change from hectic New York City. Summers in the city have always been notorious for their stifling heat and humidity. The Burr women often escaped the oppressiveness by visiting his farm, about 20 miles (32 km) north of the city. Theodosia and her mother had great fun hiking, swimming, and learning about life on the farm. Theodosia was expected to continue her study routine while there. Her mother thought the change of environment and healthy country air contributed to Theo's success during their summers there.

Burr wanted his daughter to learn horseback riding at the Pelham farm, and during one visit when Theodosia was eight, Frederick set aside a horse for her. But their mother thought the other children would feel left out. Instead, for amusement, they all went riding through the countryside in a cart pulled by a different horse. Theodosia's mother remembered, "We have a good plain Dutch wagon, that I prefer to a carriage when at Pelham, as the exercise is much better. We ride in numbers and are well jolted. 'Tis the most powerful exercise I know. No spring seats; but, like so many pigs we bundle together on straw. Four miles [6.5 km] are equal to twenty [32 km]."

Theodosia made significant advances in her studies, including French. She added French phrases and entire paragraphs in her letters to her father. Under her mother's guidance, she translated the Declaration of Independence into French. To reward her efforts, her father shopped in Westchester, New York, for a French book to bring her. He described his adventure:

I rose up from the sofa, and rubbing my head—"What book shall I buy for her?" I said to myself. "She reads so much and so rapidly that it is not easy to find proper and amusing French books for her." I went into one bookseller's shop after another. I found plenty of fairy tales and such nonsense. "These," said I "will never do. Her understanding begins to be above such things," but I could see nothing that I would offer with pleasure to an intelligent, well-informed girl of nine years old. I persevered. At last I found it. I found the very thing I sought. I must present it with my own hand.

By 1792, Theo wrote regularly to her father and he to her. Her mother was often too sick to write. Historians believe she likely had the beginnings of stomach cancer. Theodosia became the primary communicator to her father about her mother's condition and medical treatments. She also was the link between Burr and her mother's doctors. These were great responsibilities for a young girl, and they drew father and daughter closer together. Theodosia never expressed her worries about her mother in her letters to her father. Father and daughter, in their written correspondence, did not discuss their fears of losing the wife and mother they both loved.

Meanwhile, Burr worried that his daughter's education was unbalanced. He also expressed concern that her tutor was not coming to the home regularly. "I would by no means have her writing and arithmetic neglected. It is the part of her education which is of the most present importance. If Shepherd [the tutor] will not attend her in the house, another must be had; but I had rather pay him double than employ another."

ALWAYS A TEACHER

In addition to Theodosia's tutors, Burr served as a constant teacher and used his letters to his daughter as an opportunity to critique her spelling and grammar. He also challenged her to learn the uses and preparations of medicines. When she was eleven, he wrote, "You write acurate for accurate, laudnam for laudanum; intirely for entirely; this last word, indeed, is spelled both ways but entirely is the most usual and the most proper. Continue to use all these words in your next letter, that I may see you know the true spelling. And tell me what is laudanum? Where and how made? And what are its effects?" (Laudanum is a tincture, or extract, of opium. About 10 percent opium, it was used to reduce pain.)

Burr believed the keys to his own success were the disciplinary study habits he had developed when he was young. He instructed

---

Plan of the Journal.

16th December, 1793.

Learned 230 lines, which finished **Horace.** Heigh-ho for Terence and the Greek grammar to-morrow.

Practised two hours less **thirty-five minutes,** which I begged off.

Hewlett (dancing-master) did not come.

Began Gibbon last evening. I find he requires as much study and attention as Horace; so I shall not rank the reading of *him* among amusements.

Skated an hour; fell twenty times, and find the advantage of a hard head and

Ma better—dined with us at table, and is still sitting up and free from pain.

Your affectionate papa,

A. Burr.

This sample of a study journal that Aaron Burr sent to his daughter in 1783 encourages her to keep similar records of her own studies.

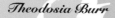

Theodosia to keep a journal of her daily activities and send it to him every Monday. He wanted his daughter to adopt a routine that would bring her future success. When the journal she supplied did not meet his expectations, he sent her an example he had created specifically for her to follow. From it, historians see that, like boys her age, she was already learning to read Latin and was studying Horace, an ancient Roman poet, and Terence, an ancient Roman playwright. She was also studying a classic eighteenth-century six-volume work about Roman history called *The History of the Decline and Fall of the Roman Empire,* by English historian Edward Gibbon. These were some of the prerequisites for college admission. And for fun, she went skating on a local pond with friends.

Burr encouraged Theodosia to expand her knowledge of different subjects. He challenged her to learn the names of all of the flowers in the garden and send them to him. He encouraged her to try writing fiction. When he received her responses, he praised her efforts and lovingly encouraged her to do even more.

Burr also offered advice from his own experience as a person who had tried and failed, tried again, and ultimately succeeded. He told her not to worry about a problem that was difficult to solve, but to try for a time, move on to something else, and then try again another time. One bad day was not a reason to be discouraged, he wrote, but an event from which to learn.

And when it came to friends, he advised Theodosia to seek solid friendships that would mature over time rather than friendships with those who sought her because of her beauty or wealth. Friends, he said, that you gain and never lose.

4

A Scandalous Book

The very constitution of civil governments has put almost insuperable [impossible to overcome] obstacles in the way to prevent the cultivation of the female understanding.

—Mary Wollstonecraft, author, 1792

While Burr was serving in the US Senate, he bought a copy of a book that had caused a sensation in London. He stayed up all night to read it and sent it to his wife with an enthusiastic letter expressing great admiration for the book's author. The book was *A Vindication of the Rights of Woman*, published in London in 1792. Young Theodosia didn't know it at the time, but the book would have a huge impact on her future. The author, Mary Wollstonecraft, was the wife of radical philosopher William Godwin and the mother of Mary Shelley (who would later write the classic novel *Frankenstein*). The Godwins, unlike most English people and Americans, believed in the equal treatment of women in education, family, society, and law. In her book, Wollstonecraft discussed the state of womanhood in England at the time.

In the eighteenth century, women were considered childlike in intellectual ability, incapable of rational or deep thinking. Women were encouraged to develop their sensibility, or experience of the world,

John Opie painted this portrait of English author Mary Wollstonecraft in 1797. Her belief in women's equality was considered radical at the time. The Burrs fully supported the philosophy of equal rights for women.

through sensory (emotional and physical) stimulation rather than through reason. Wollstonecraft wrote that sensibility made women unable to cope with life as discerning beings, unable to rely on intellect and judgment. They were therefore always overwhelmed by feelings and often unable to make smart, sound decisions. She wrote, "Their senses are inflamed, and their understandings neglected; consequently they become the prey of their sense, delicately termed sensibility, and are blown about by every momentary gust of feeling."

In her introduction to her book, Wollstonecraft addressed her female readers as intelligent, thinking beings, able to understand the philosophies presented in her book, rather than as children. She wrote, "My own sex, I hope, will excuse me, if I treat them like rational creatures, instead of flattering their fascinating graces [looks and personality], and viewing them as if they were in a state of perpetual childhood, unable to stand alone."

The central theme of Wollstonecraft's book is that women would be better mothers and wives, able to make sound decisions and contribute to society, if they were educated in the same manner as men. She suggested a school system that would put girls and boys in the same classes so they would learn together, at the same pace. Her revolutionary and controversial ideas were met with hostility from readers on both sides of the Atlantic.

Burr was overcome with admiration for Wollstonecraft. He described the book as "a work of genius" and wondered why no one in Philadelphia seemed to be interested in such groundbreaking ideas. Even though the book was a sensation in London, Burr could not find anyone in the capital, a city filled with America's greatest thinkers, who wanted to read it.

In a letter to his wife, he wrote about society women of Philadelphia and the effects of their fashionable education. He believed it victimized and objectified them. He thought that scholarly training would help women achieve their best in life and would be much better for them, their families, and the nation. Women could be, he said, as much a vital national resource as men and ought to be educated to the best of their ability. He described Philadelphia women as frivolous and mindless and wrote in strong terms that he would prefer death for his daughter rather than a life like theirs. "If I could foresee that Theo would become a mere fashionable woman, with all the attendant frivolity [silliness] and vacuity [emptiness] of mind, adorned with whatever grace and allurement, I would earnestly pray God to take her forthwith hence."

The Burrs kept a picture of Mary Wollstonecraft on the mantle from that time forward.

"CHILDREN OF A LARGER GROWTH"

Wollstonecraft's book was a reaction to another book, *Letters to His Son on the Art of Becoming a Man of the World and a Gentleman*, which had come out twenty years before hers. Written by Philip Stanhope, Earl of

Chesterfield, and published in London in 1774, it compiled letters Chesterfield had sent to his sons. The letters contained advice for his sixteen-year-old son, who had been born outside of marriage, on how to be a successful gentleman in polite society. It became the basis for social interactions between men and women of the eighteenth century in England as well as in the United States. In one of the letters, Chesterfield wrote, "Women, then are only children of a larger growth; they have an entertaining tattle, and sometimes wit. A man of sense only trifles with them, plays with them, humors and flatters them, as he does with a sprightly forward child; but he neither consults them about, nor trusts them with serious matters."

Allan Ramsay painted this portrait of Philip Stanhope, fourth Earl of Chesterfield, in 1765. The earl held conventional attitudes about women, and his writings guided British and American attitudes toward gender relations in the eighteenth century.

Yet with the American Revolution, women's roles had begun to change slowly. During the years that American men were away at war, participating in the new Congress or traveling as diplomats, their wives ran the family businesses. Abigail Adams—wife of future president John Adams—wrote to her husband in her famous "Remember the Ladies" letter of 1776 that women would be just as capable after the war as they were during the conflict.

Mary Wollstonecraft strongly objected to Chesterfield's description of women and the treatment of women of her time. The Burrs often

"Remember the Ladies"

Abigail Adams (1744–1818), the wife of President John Adams, wrote about life for women in the eighteenth century and the problems and limitations they faced. She was an advocate of education for women, property rights for women (which did not exist then), and a role for women that was more than companionship for men. In March 1776, she wrote a letter to her husband while he was attending a meeting of the Second Continental Congress in Philadelphia. This Congress declared independence from Great Britain and worked over a period of years to set up the laws of the new United States. Her letter is remembered as the "Remember the Ladies" letter. In it, she wrote, "In the new code of laws . . . remember the ladies, and be more generous and favorable to them than your ancestors. Do not put such unlimited power into the hands of the Husbands. Remember all Men would be tyrants if they could." The letter did not influence those laws at that time, but it set the stage for changes to come.

Benjamin Blythe painted this portrait of Abigail Adams when she was First Lady (1797–1801). The fichu, or scarf, she is wearing was popular in the eighteenth and early nineteenth centuries. It was sometimes used to fill in low necklines, and women either tied or pinned them into place.

wrote in their letters about these contradictory views, debating the merits of Chesterfield versus Wollstonecraft. In his letters to his daughter, Burr relies on a mixture of Chesterfield's rules of discipline and study (meant for boys) and Wollstonecraft's theory of women's ability to be thoughtful and independent. He expected both from his daughter.

CARING FOR HER MOTHER

Theodosia's mother continued to grow worse as the months of 1793 passed. Dr. Samuel Bard, who treated her, was a prominent man of medicine. In the 1760s, he had founded the first medical school in New York. He also founded the Columbia University College of Physicians and Surgeons and served as dean of Columbia College. Meanwhile, when Burr was in Philadelphia, he consulted Dr. Benjamin Rush, the nation's preeminent doctor. Bard and Rush recommended different treatments, ranging from hemlock pills to laudanum. As an extreme move, Rush even recommended mercury treatments. They tried dietary changes, sometimes excluding dairy, occasionally focusing on vegetarian meals and sometimes meat. Rush suggested it was best for the patient to eat whatever her stomach would tolerate so that she did not become anemic. (Anemia is the lack of iron in the body's bloodstream and often occurs in patients with stomach cancers.) In early 1794, because his wife was not improving, Burr considered resigning from the Senate to care for her. She told him to "omit all thoughts of leaving Congress."

> **"The mother of my Theo was the best woman and finest lady I have ever known."**
>
> —Aaron Burr, quoted in Henry Childs Merwin, Aaron Burr, 1899

Theodosia, responsible for her mother's care, was able to continue her studies without interruption. Even with the burdens placed upon her, she excelled. Burr boasted to her that he had showed one of her letters to Rush, who could not believe it was written by a girl of less than seventeen. Burr pointed to his daughter's letters discussing medicines to praise her accomplishments and improve her knowledge. "There is not a word misspelled either in your journal or letter, which cannot be said of a single page you ever before wrote. . . . Be able, upon my arrival, to tell me the difference between an infusion [extraction of plant compounds or flavors in water, oil, or alcohol] and a decoction [extraction of herbs or plants by boiling them in water]."

5

Natalie de l'Age
de Volude

In order that Theodosia might have the advantage of conversing in French with a Frenchwoman, Miss Natalie de l'Age became a member of Colonel Burr's family.

—*Charles Felton Pidgin, Theodosia Burr biographer*

In the 1790s, as the health of Theo's mother was declining, New York's French population was growing. The newcomers were fleeing the violence of the French Revolution (1789–1799). France had been an unwavering supporter of the American cause during the American Revolution, sending money, soldiers, and the powerful French navy to help fight the British (a historic enemy of the French). New York returned the favor by welcoming French refugees to the growing city.

Three decorated French officers who had served under George Washington during the American Revolution already lived in New York. John Vacher was a doctor. Stephen Rochefontaine was an engineer, first commander of the US Army Corps of Engineers, and founder of the engineering school at the Military Academy

Charles Balthazar Julien Févret de Saint-Mémin made these engravings of Theodosia Burr (*left*) and her companion and friend Natalie de l'Age de Volude (*right*) in 1796. The artworks are in the National Portrait Gallery at the Smithsonian Institution in Washington, DC.

at West Point. Pierre L'Enfant was an architect who designed the altar at Saint Paul's Chapel (the site of Washington's postinaugural church service) and Federal Hall on Wall Street, where Washington took his presidential oath. L'Enfant later planned the city of Washington, DC.

A NEAR-CONSTANT COMPANION

Ten-year-old Natalie de l'Age de Volude, her governess Madame de Senat, and de Senat's young daughter (historians do not know their first names) were among the French refugees newly arrived in crowded New York City on a cold, wet day in the early 1790s. They were far from their home in Paris. They didn't know a soul, and the two girls didn't speak any English.

Natalie was born at the palace at Versailles, France, the main residence of France's king and queen. Her mother and father were French nobility. King Louis XVI and Queen Marie Antoinette were her godparents. When revolutionaries arrested and imprisoned the

The French Revolution

In the eighteenth century, European peoples—like Americans before them—began to overthrow the monarchies that ruled them. These conflicts were part of a movement that historians call the Age of Revolution (1774–1849). During this era, nations chose democratic rule over that of kings and queens. During the French Revolution, the people of France overthrew the monarchy of King Louis XVI and Queen Marie Antoinette. The peasants and lower classes had suffered starvation, poverty, and violent abuse under the reign of France's aristocratic class. While France's nobility lived on large estates, wore expensive clothes and jewelry, and enjoyed lives of luxury and leisure, the peasants often lived in the misery of extreme poverty. In Paris on July 14, 1789, peasants stormed the Bastille, a prison and symbol of the nobility's political power, and released the prisoners. It marked the beginning of the French Revolution.

During the Reign of Terror (1793–1794), French revolutionaries and peasants expressed their fury at the nobility by putting them on public trial. There, crowds insulted, jeered at, and humiliated them. Most were found guilty and executed at the guillotine, where an executioner would drop the device's large, sharp blade to cut off the prisoner's head—in public, before cheering crowds. Among the executed were the French king and queen, members of their court, and other aristocrats. About three hundred thousand people were arrested, and seventeen thousand were put on trial and executed at the guillotine. And twenty-three thousand were killed without a trial or died while in prison. Some members of the French aristocracy fled to safety in England and the United States.

king and queen, Natalie's mother, Stephanie d'Amblimont, Marquise de l'Age de Volude, separated her children and sent them to different locations. She hoped they would survive and be reunited. She sent Natalie and her governess to the United States, and she and her husband fled. Natalie was in a new land, with a different language and customs, away from her loving family whom she might never see again. It was a heavy burden for a little girl who had never known a day of hardship before.

This 1789 watercolor by Jean-Pierre Houël shows peasants storming the Bastille prison in Paris. The event marked the beginning of the French Revolution.

The French Revolution was controversial in the United States, where anti-Federalists such as Thomas Jefferson initially supported it. They felt it followed the spirit of the American Revolution, but they changed their position when they learned of the violence and social anarchy that was occurring. Federalists such as John Adams and Alexander Hamilton opposed the revolution. They condemned the violence as an assault on civilized society and religious faith. Hamilton called it a "disgusting spectacle" and a "plan to disorganize the human mind itself."

Madame de Senat eventually opened a school—the DeSenat Seminary—for the children of French refugees living in the city. She invited the children of New York's premier families seeking a French education that would set their children apart from other families, as part of an international society. Theodosia Burr was one of them. Her father had offered Madame de Senat the use of one of the family properties—a townhome on Partition Street—as a residence and location for the DeSenat Seminary.

Natalie and Theodosia were only six months apart in age. They quickly became best friends and adopted sisters. When Burr was away from home, Madame de S. (as she was known in letters between father and daughter) looked after Theodosia with motherly affection while guiding her in learning French. Madame de S. and Natalie also helped Theo master the intricacies of etiquette and French dance styles.

In Burr's letters, he instructed Theodosia to copy Natalie's manners in every way. This would ensure Theodosia's mastery of the finest details of French language, manners, and society. Theodosia would learn naturally, from her very best friend. In turn, Natalie would learn from Theodosia about how to fit into life in New York. As they matured and learned from each other Burr and Madame de S. observed and guided their progress.

Natalie was happy to have a new home and was grateful for Burr's generosity. Burr developed an affection for her, just as he had for his stepchildren. He encouraged Theodosia to spend as much time as possible with Madame's French friends as well. "You may, indeed it is my wish that you should, visit with Madame de S. all her French acquaintance. Do you continue to preserve Madame De S's good opinion of your talents for the harp? And do you find that you converse with more facility in the French?" Theodosia was learning to play the harp because young women were often called upon to demonstrate their skills on this instrument at dinner parties and other social gatherings.

Socially, Theodosia and Natalie were typical upper-class teenagers in the United States of their era. They went shopping, attended balls, danced in ballets, went to parties, and socialized throughout the city. A Saturday night in summer might find them at a ball at one of the town's elaborate, English-style pleasure gardens. Pleasure gardens were all the rage and were often named and designed after famous ones in London. New York had two: Vauxhall and Ranelagh.

Dancing

Ballroom dancing was a central part of social life. The two most popular dances of Theodosia's time were the quadrille and cotillion. Both were elaborate dances that required many hours of practice to perfect. Theodosia had a dance master who came to the home along with a violinist (recorded music did not exist then) to instruct her. Madame de Senat worked with her on the fine points of how to hold her head gracefully, where to place her hands, and how to glide smoothly along the dance floor.

The quadrille was a dance for four couples arranged in a rectangle. The couples moved through five different patterns, each one a mini dance of its own. In the cotillion, also for four pairs, the participants formed a square. Dancers moved through a series of patterns, or changes. The lead couple or a conductor called out the steps at random or sometimes as a prearranged set. Changes included circles, chains, and switching dance partners. Originating in France, it was the forerunner of American square dancing.

This illustration, with its humorous caption, shows a conductor (*with violin at left*) and a group of dancers practicing the steps of the trenis, a type of quadrille. Theodosia would have mastered this popular French dance style. British publisher J. Sidebotham printed the image in London in the 1820s.

Pleasure Gardens

Before movie theaters, concerts, and sports arenas, people went to pleasure gardens for entertainment. They were highly popular in the eighteenth and nineteenth centuries in the United States, England, and Europe. Each garden was unique, with its own layout of fountains, statues, shrubs, and flower gardens. Some included band shells, zoos, theater stages, and amusement rides.

Gardens competed for customers by showcasing famous bands and theater groups as well as the hottest trends in food and drink. Some also offered ice-skating in the winter to provide year-round entertainment. New York's two most popular pleasure gardens during Theodosia's time were Vauxhall and Ranelagh. Both were named for two magnificent and popular pleasure gardens in London.

This unattributed and undated illustration from the early nineteenth century depicts the risqué merriment of pleasure gardens. Tremendously popular, these sites were one of the few places where the white middle class would encounter people of color (usually as entertainers). They were also a place of debauchery, where men drank too much, fought, and caroused with women.

The gardens were places where teen girls and young women could see their friends and show off their beautiful dresses, fashionable hairdos, dancing skills, and excellent French manners. It was a way for them to meet equally well-dressed and well-mannered young men, flirting and mingling under the watchful eyes of chaperones such as Madame de Senat.

When they weren't in New York, the Burrs lived at Richmond Hill, a sprawling estate north of the city on the Hudson River. In the mornings, Theodosia and Natalie liked to take horses from the stable and ride across the property to the river. They gazed out across the water, imagining trips to exotic places on the ships passing by. On a hot day, they might swim in the river's cold waters. They were each other's closest confidants. They laughed, joked, and shared scandalous stories of secret flirtations with young men they liked. Both girls were welcomed and admired in New York's social circles. At the same time, they were both curiosities: Natalie because she was French and Theodosia because of her unusual education. They supported and encouraged each other through awkward and difficult times.

Besides her busy social schedule and studies at DeSenat Seminary, Theodosia had to keep up her studies. She read Homer's *Odyssey* and *Iliad* (in Greek) and summarized them in letters to her father. Burr encouraged her to try her hand at writing fiction and requested that she compose something for him in the style of a current favorite novel. She capably balanced growing up culturally a young woman with the scholastic accomplishments expected of a young man.

6

The Young Mistress

With his wife gone, Burr focused all of his love on his daughter.
—Richard Côté, Theodosia Burr biographer

Theodosia Prévost Burr died in May 1794. She was buried in the graveyard at Trinity Church in New York City. Her daughter was just short of her eleventh birthday. She lost her constant companion, a loving mother who nurtured and guided her through her early years. Theodosia was closest emotionally to her. Although she loved, looked up to, and respected her father, he was away so much that the same emotional bond had not formed between them.

The loss of his wife was difficult for Burr. He had shared his most intimate thoughts with her and looked to her for direction. Burr loved her more than any woman he would ever meet. Had she lived to continue guiding him, his political life might have been completely different.

Father and daughter were alone. They would have to find their way forward together. The death drew them closer than any other father and daughter were known to be at that time.

MOVING FORWARD

The year after his wife's death, Burr decided to lease a country home in what is now the West Village of New York City. Until that home was ready, Burr, his daughter, and the household staff moved to a newly built home on Partition Street. (The street later became part of Fulton Street.) It was on a tree-lined street on the west side of Broadway, a step up from their old neighborhood. The house was a spacious brick townhome, two stories high, with room for a law office. Burr wrote to Theodosia from Philadelphia in January 1795, "Our home in Partition-Street . . . pleases me much."

In November Theodosia made her first trip out of New York to accompany her father to Philadelphia and stay with him for part of his term in the US Senate. This was the first of many political trips with her father. During their visit, she and her father socialized with some of the most notable families of Philadelphia society, where she was finally able to meet Dr. Rush in person. The young girl, with her mix of masculine education and French manners, was a sensation. Theodosia endeared herself to everyone she met. Her father was immensely proud of his Miss Burr.

An unusual decision for the time, Burr also brought his daughter to hear President Washington address both houses of Congress. Theodosia stood among her father's colleagues, which included some of the nation's most respected thinkers: Vice President John Adams, Secretary of State Timothy Pickering, Chief Justice of the Supreme Court John Rutledge, and many others. Theo wrote to her brother, John Bartow, about the president's speech to Congress that "I went to hear the president's speech to both houses of Congress he was dressed in a complete suit of black velvet. I heard very little and understood less."

She also wrote that two men at the inn where they were staying had claimed they were robbed, one of thirty-five dollars and the other of ten. The guests assumed Burr servants Thomas and Alexis were

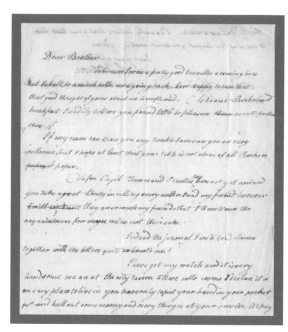

Theodosia wrote regularly to her brother John Bartow. In this letter from 1795, she describes having heard President George Washington deliver a speech to Congress in Philadelphia. It also recounts the charges of theft against two of the Burr servants who accompanied her and her father on the trip.

the culprits because they were black. Theodosia told her brother how proud she was of the servants. She wrote that Alexis "defended himself with great gravity and eloquence." Thomas, on the other hand, told the crowd that had gathered at the inn, "I wish I was as sure of going to heaven as I am that he [Alexis] did not steal the money." The two guests threatened to call the constable (police) and send Thomas and Alexis to jail. But in the end "not a word did [the accusers] say to papa."

Theo closed her letter with a paragraph in French, sending regards to her brother from Alexis. In her letter, she refers to the servant as "Citoyen Alexis" (French for "Citizen Alexis"), a play on words, to demonstrate her knowledge of French politics and the new ideas about equality that would lead to the French Revolution.

RICHMOND HILL

By 1796, Burr and his daughter were living most of the time at their massive, verdant estate at Richmond Hill. They occasionally used their home in the city on Partition Street. Many prominent families maintained townhomes within the city and country estates to the north. When she was fourteen, Theodosia became mistress of the home, near modern-day Charlton and Varick Streets on the western side of Manhattan Island. The home had a long, venerable history. In 1776 it briefly had been General Washington's headquarters. During the revolution, British commander Guy Carleton lived there. It was also home to the United States' first vice president, John Adams, and his family. First Lady Abigail Adams, especially, loved the estate and wrote to her sister about its beauty.

John Adams was an American statesman, attorney, diplomat, writer, and Founding Father. He served as the first vice president of the United States from 1789 to 1797. American artist Gilbert Stuart painted this portrait of Adams in about 1800, when Adams was president of the United States. Theodosia met and knew Adams because he was one of her father's political colleagues.

An undated watercolor depicts the elegance and calm of the Burr home on Richmond Hill. The only structure that remains in the twenty-first century is the stable house, where horses were kept, at 17 Barrow Street in Lower Manhattan. Visitors to New York City can see the stable house and eat at the restaurant that occupies the site.

From one of the balconies of the Richmond Hill house, Theodosia could see the Hudson River in the distance and all the way to New Jersey on the opposite side. The house was elevated on a hill. Spread out between it and the river were flower gardens, shrubs, forest, fields, and pasture. Bestevaer's Killetje, or Minetta Creek, ran through the property's 160 acres (65 ha) and emptied into the Hudson. Burr had workers dam a portion of the creek to form a pond for skating in the winter. Swimming in the river was a popular summer pastime.

The house was a two-and-one-half story wood-framed mansion with a portico (front entrance) supported by columns, decorative exterior moldings, and porch railings. Inside, a broad staircase with a mahogany railing led to the second floor. The home was filled with the most luxurious furnishings of the time. Most admired by visitors, though, was the extensive library. Burr had been collecting books since his days as a student at Princeton and spent years acquiring more on his American, British, and European travels.

Bathing Machines

In the eighteenth century, women and girls who wanted to go swimming in the Hudson River on a hot summer day changed clothes in bathing machines. Girls and women could change privately from street clothes to bathing gowns in this walled and roofed wooden cart. The swimmer bought a ticket, presented it to a worker called a dipper, and entered the bathing machine. A swimmer changed clothes while the dipper pulled the cart into the water. When she was in her modest bathing costume (a dresslike outfit that covered the body from neck to ankles), the swimmer opened the door and walked down a few steps into the water. The cart remained in the water while the woman or girl swam. Then she entered the bathing machine. The dipper pulled it back to shore, and she changed into street clothes. Bathing machines were used until about the 1920s. Then beaches set up stationary changing rooms for men and women, and men started wearing bathing suits rather than swimming nude.

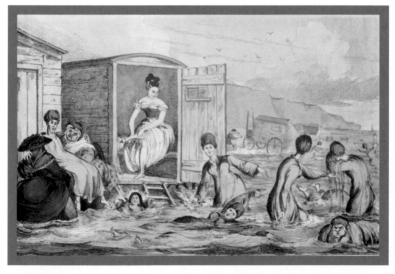

William Heath made this illustration of bathing machines in Brighton, England, in 1829. In the United States, men sometimes used bathing machines too, but they more commonly swam in the nude. Men and women usually swam separately.

In September 1795, when she was thirteen, Theodosia received notice from her father, working in Philadelphia, to prepare Richmond Hill for the family of his friend Colonel Ward. That year a lethal epidemic of yellow fever swept through New York City. Infectious diseases were difficult, if not impossible, to contain because of poor public sanitation, and antibiotics and vaccinations had not yet been invented. Epidemics of yellow fever, typhus, cholera, and smallpox were common. Always generous, Burr offered the safety of his estate outside the city to the colonel's family.

Theodosia enthusiastically took on the task of advising servants Anthony and Peggy to prepare the extra rooms with clean linens, washbasins, and chamber pots for the guests. (In the centuries before

Yellow Fever Epidemic of 1795

New York suffered one of its worst epidemics of yellow fever, a viral disease spread by mosquito bites, in 1795. The symptoms include fever, chills, loss of appetite, nausea, diarrhea (sometimes bloody), muscle pain, and headaches. The disease was sometimes fatal. Without effective treatments and a lack of sanitary conditions, it spread rapidly. New York's doctors disagreed about a proper treatment, and newspapers published conflicting advice. City leaders tried to downplay the seriousness to prevent panic, but people who had another place to live fled the city for safety.

Someone on board a ship from the Caribbean region reportedly brought the epidemic to the city in July 1795. By September it had spread throughout New York City. Governor John Jay, trying to reduce its spread, issued a proclamation banning all vessels from the West Indies (a group of islands in the North Atlantic Ocean and Caribbean Sea) from approaching the city. The governor also established a health committee to deal with the epidemic, and the committee issued a statement on the importance of "the cleanliness of the streets, yards, cellars, and markets, and the removal of all putrescent [rotting] matter, are objects of very great importance, and ought to be particularly attended to."

indoor plumbing, families used small ceramic indoor pots as toilets. Servants emptied them every day to keep them clean.) She made sure that Thomas, the cook, had enough food to feed everyone and that all would be comfortable and welcoming for her guests. Theodosia handled her responsibilities without complaint. One of Burr's friends described her as "the engaging mistress of his household."

Like any loving father, Burr worried about his daughter while he was away. During the yellow fever epidemic, he learned that Theodosia was still spending time in the city at the house on Partition Street. "Why are you still in town? I am very dissatisfied with it," he wrote. He went on to instruct her to take a pile of books and head to Frederick's farm to safety.

A UNIQUE HOUSEHOLD

Theodosia had plenty of help managing Richmond Hill while her father was absent. The Burr household had a full staff of servants, formerly enslaved, who worked to keep things running smoothly. In their letters to each other, Theo and her father most often mention Tom, Burr's valet Alexis, and Peggy Garten, who supervised day-to-day household needs of the home. (Historians do not know the last names of every servant in the Burr household, but they do know some.)

The Burr staff came and went freely and were well respected in the community. Burr wanted everyone in his household to be educated, including the servants. In a letter to Theodosia, he mentioned that Tom had injured his foot and should take the opportunity to spend his time in the library. This would have been a radical suggestion at the time, when servants were

> **"Poor Tom! I hope you take good care of him. If he is confined by his leg, he must pay the greater attention to his reading and writing."**
>
> —Aaron Burr to Theodosia, upon hearing that their servant Thomas had injured his leg, 1794

viewed as second-class citizens and were not expected or encouraged to pursue learning. In another letter, he tells her that French-speaking Alexis was looking forward to her teaching him to read and write in English.

In lovely penmanship and near-perfect grammar, Garten wrote directly to her employer. She explained to him that she wanted to further her education and requested permission to attend a day school. "I wish to beg a favour of you; please to grant it. I have found there is a day-school, kept by an elderly man and his wife, near to our house, and if [you are] willing that I should go to it for two months, I think it would be of great service to me, and at the same time I will not neglect my work in the house, if you please, sir."

Burr enthusiastically agreed and promptly paid the tuition for her. Later, Garten updated him on her progress and told him she was teaching Nancy, another member of the household staff, what she was learning there. "I go to the school . . . and I like the teacher very much. He pays great attention to my learning, and I have teached Nancy her letters ever since you have been gone, which I think will be of as much service to her as if she went to school."

DISTINGUISHED GUESTS

Burr entertained the country's most prestigious leaders at Richmond Hill. They included prominent figures such as Alexander Hamilton, James Madison, and Thomas Jefferson as well as noted New Yorkers such as author Washington Irving (a regular visitor) and city mayors Marinus Willett and Edward Livingston. Visitors from France included the future King Louis Philippe, who came to Richmond Hill with his two younger brothers. Theodosia met and hosted them all.

Theodosia helped plan formal occasions and participated in them at her father's side. She managed the household staff, relayed her father's wishes to her tutors, and handled household expenses—including payments to her teachers—in her father's absences. Her father reminded her in a letter, "You must pay off Meance and Hewlet for their attendance on you. . . . They must be paid regularly at the end of each month. Tell Mr Martell that I request that all the time he can spare you be devoted to Latin."

A STATE DINNER

On a winter day in February 1797, an unusual and distinguished visitor interrupted thirteen-year-old Theodosia's daily schedule of study. Joseph Brant was on his way to his home in Canada after spending time in Philadelphia. Brant, or Thayendanegea, was a Mohawk chief of the six Iroquois Nations. He was also one of Aaron Burr's friends. Brant carried a letter of introduction from Burr. The letter said,

> *This will be handed to you by Colonel Brant, the celebrated Indian Chief. I am sure that you and Natalie will be happy in the opportunity of seeing a man so much renowned. He is a man of education—speaks and writes the English perfectly—and has seen much of Europe and America. Receive him with respect and hospitality. He has daughters—if you could think of some little present to send to one of them—a pair of earrings, for example,—it would please him. You may talk to him very freely.*

Theodosia was living at the Partition Street townhome. She politely welcomed her guest and went about planning a formal dinner at Richmond Hill on his behalf. Brant found lodgings in the city and stayed for a time, socializing and meeting with the city's business leaders and others.

Welcoming Brant was as distinguished an honor as welcoming a diplomat from England, Spain, or France. The formal dinner at Richmond Hill would be comparable to holding a state dinner.

Chief Brant and the Six Iroquois Nations

Joseph Brant, Thayendanegea, was a member of the Iroquois Confederacy, an alliance of Indian nations, and a political and military leader during the American Revolution. Brant was a member of the Mohawk Nation, one of the six tribes of the Confederacy, which also included the Onondaga, Oneida, Cayuga, Seneca, and Tuscarora nations. The six nations referred to themselves as the Haudenosaunee, which means "People of the Longhouse." Longhouses were long, wide houses covered in wood and bark for a group of related families. Confederacy lands were vast, stretching from Lake Champlain and the Hudson River in the east, the Niagara River–Lake Erie area in the west, the Delaware River and the central Pennsylvania mountains to the south, and the Saint Lawrence River to the north.

Joseph Brant was the subject of many portraits during his lifetime. George Romney created this formal portrait in oil of Brant in England in 1776. Brant is pictured wearing English fashion—a white ruffled shirt and a silver ornamental collar known as a gorget—as well as a traditional Mohawk blanket over his left arm and a tomahawk in the other hand.

Brant was educated at Moor's Indian Charity School in Connecticut, which later became Dartmouth College of New Hampshire. He learned to speak, read, and write English and studied other academic subjects as well. He learned farming, math, and the classics of European literature. He spoke at least three and possibly all Six Nations languages. Brant planned to attend King's College in New York. But because of hostilities against the Haudenosaunee by the British government of the New York colony, he was unable to. Later, he traveled to England, where he met King George III, and from there visited the European continent.

Four Haudenosaunee tribes, including the Mohawk, fought with the British against the American colonies during the Revolutionary War. After the war, their lands became part of the United States. During Theodosia Burr's time, Brant had settled in what is Ontario, Canada.

> **"She received the . . . Chief with all the courtesy and hospitality suggested; and, young as she was, she performed the honors of her father's house in a manner that must have been as gratifying to her absent parent as it was creditable to herself."**
>
> —William Leete Stone, biographer of Joseph Brant, 1838

Theodosia Burr, in her father's absence, would sit at the head of the table, all eyes on her, as she performed the duties of the honored hostess. (Her father was in Philadelphia, serving in the US Senate, and could not attend the dinner.)

Theodosia carefully planned the menu, chose the wine from the wine cellar, selected the china and silverware, planned the seating arrangement for her guests, and wrote proper invitations to some of the city's most prominent residents. On the night of the dinner, carriages lined up at Richmond Hill to drop off the distinguished guests. Theodosia formally greeted everyone in the parlor and personally introduced Brant to each visitor. When dinner was ready, she directed the guests to the dining room, sat at the head of the table, and guided the dinner conversation with poise and flawless etiquette. After dinner, the group returned to the parlor for casual conversation.

One of the dinner guests that night was Rector Benjamin Moore of the Episcopal (Trinity) Church in New York City. Moore became bishop of the church a few years later. Also present was Samuel Bard, who had treated Theodosia's mother during her long illness. Another doctor, David Hosack, attended the dinner as well.

The dinner was a great success. Theodosia, triumphant, emerged as one of the preeminent hostesses of the city. It set the foundation for her entrée into the top echelon of American society. Brant was impressed with and remembered his young hostess. He left her with an invitation to visit him at his home in Canada. Years later, after she married, the newlyweds accepted his offer and visited him in Ontario.

7

"The First Gentlewoman of Her Time"

Her person was small, while to its enchanted symmetry and expression of countenance illuminated by vast reading and general knowledge and flashing wit made her the ruling spirit to every circle.
—John Davis, English visitor to New York City, 1798

Gifted as she was, Theodosia was not immune to the awkwardness and insecurity of being a teenager. Added to that, her father's notoriety and public expectation of how she should look, speak, and behave put even more pressure on her to be perfect. Everyone knew about her experimental education, placing her under a social microscope of observation. Some people encouraged her, while others hoped she would fail. Theodosia had to navigate those dangerous waters carefully, or the slightest mistake might be disastrous for her social standing.

How would she figure out who she was? Would she ever be more than Aaron Burr's daughter or the girl with the masculine education? How would she step out of her powerful father's shadow to become

Theodosia Burr in her own right? And even if she did master the strict intellectual and social requirements of her time, how would she use them?

The United States of the late eighteenth century, free of the old constraints of British law and tradition, offered new opportunities for men. A person no longer needed to be from an aristocratic family to succeed. Men had so many opportunities open to them: lawyer, doctor, political leader, college professor, merchant, banker, ship captain, farmer, and much more. But for women, the opportunities were still only for a good marriage and respectable place in society. Through marriage, women could influence their husbands and other men in their social circles. The only professions open to women were dressmaker, governess, and domestic servant, all far beneath Theodosia's status. With an education worthy of a senator or president, Theodosia could find her place only through marriage—and to a husband looking for a companion of equal intellect and scholarship.

A typical lady's life must have seemed stifling and boring to Theodosia. What intellectual satisfaction would she find sitting in a parlor in the afternoon drinking tea, doing needlework, and chatting about the latest town gossip with female friends? Instead, her mind was on the exciting politics of the new United States, philosophy, Greek mythology, and ancient history. She was likely more interested in joining a room of educated young men who held similar interests. Yet American society was segregated by gender. After dinner, men and women often separated into different rooms to talk. Theodosia often found it difficult to fit in with women as they sat and embroidered—something she had not learned— and discussed popular social topics of the time.

UNDER PRESSURE

Theodosia came from a high-profile family. As such, she had similar experiences to those of a twenty-first-century celebrity. Her great-grandfather, Jonathan Edwards, was a household name throughout colonial America. Her well-known grandfather, the Reverend Aaron Burr Sr., founded Princeton College. Her father was a towering political figure after the American Revolution, and her mother was one of the most brilliant and socially refined women of her day.

Growing up in the confines of upper-class New York society would have been difficult. Theodosia would have had to balance the social expectations of conforming to the traditional and limited roles of a young woman against her parents' expectations that she meet educational standards typical of a boy and man. Her father's political rivals were watching her, waiting, even hoping to find some failure in her knowledge or manners. A flaw in Theodosia would provide ammunition against her father's political views and his radical theories about educating girls. The pressure not to let him down must have been stifling.

Theo's father often pushed his daughter to achieve higher and higher goals while sharply criticizing her when she fell short of his expectations. Her father's letters often criticized her. Burr wrote that she should stop slouching her shoulders, that she wasn't attentive enough to others when they spoke to her, and that she should not respond when others were critical and unkind to her.

In a letter to his daughter in 1796, he wrote, "I have often seen you at table, and other situations, pay you the utmost attention; offer you twenty civilities, while you appeared scarcely sensible that she was speaking to you. A moment's reflection will convince you that this conduct will be naturally construed into arrogance; as though you thought all that attention was due to you."

In another, he directed her to, "receive with calmness every reproof, whether made kindly or unkindly; whether just or unjust. Consider within yourself whether there has been no cause for it. If it has been groundless and unjust, nevertheless bear it with composure and even with complacency."

He also told her what foods to eat and how much of them to take when she dined socially. He wrote that she should "eat of but one dish, that a plain roast or boiled; little or no gravy or butter, and very sparingly of dessert or fruit; not more than half a glass of wine; and if more of anything to eat or drink is offered, decline it."

At times, Theodosia stopped writing to her father. But she never complained, at least in writing, about her upbringing. By all accounts of those who knew her, she was a delightful mix of her mother's kindness and father's intellect. As an adult, Theodosia Burr was called "a combination of velvet [her mother] and steel [her father]."

"A SELF-POISED WOMANHOOD"

In time, Theodosia outgrew her local tutors and began managing parts of her own education. When she was fifteen, her father wrote to her, "If your young teacher, after a week's trial, should not suit you, dismiss him on any pretence without wounding his pride." But who would be her next teachers? Her father's alma mater, Princeton, did not accept women. Neither did any other college at that time. So Burr sought out teachers to come to Richmond Hill to continue his daughter's education.

> "I shall acknowledge your advancement with gratitude and the most lively pleasure. Let me entreat you not to be discouraged. Resolve to succeed and you cannot fail."
>
> —Aaron Burr to Theodosia, sixteen, letter, 1799

Burr's contemporaries criticized him for trying to re-create himself in his daughter. Rather than let her grow and come into her own, his critics said he was stifling her, molding her into his own vision of an educated, capable woman. Others, such as his younger, distant cousin, Sara Jane Lippincott, disagreed. (Lippincott was a famous writer, who published travel and gardening books in the mid-nineteenth century under the pseudonym Grace Greenwood.) Despite her own dislike of Burr, she credited him for his views about women and described Theodosia in glowing terms. Writing about him long after his death, she said,

> Aaron Burr . . . was certainly in advance of the men of his time in his ideas on the capacity and education of women. . . . There was no namby-pamby sentimentality in his method of training a clever, ambitious girl. He reared his daughter, Theodosia, to be the companion and equal of men of the highest intelligence and the most liberal culture— philosophers and statesmen. In his intense fatherly love and pride, he gave to her development and instruction the most watchful care and patient labor. The result was, I doubt not, all he wished for—a strong, pure, proud, self-poised womanhood, beautiful and gracious.

A LITERARY SALON

In Theodosia's mid-teens, her father returned to Richmond Hill. His term in the US Senate completed, he was back in New York and active in local and national politics. Theodosia took her place at her father's side, the position her mother once filled, as his political adviser, companion, and confidant. Theodosia spent time with her father's political allies, who supported Thomas Jefferson and the Anti-Federalists. She participated in conversations with New York governor George Clinton, Mayor Marinus Willet, John Peter Van Ness, Peter Irving, and Peter's famous brother, Washington Irving.

It was customary that young, literate, society women such as Theodosia would establish a salon. A salon was a regular social gathering of eminent people, including intellectuals, writers, and artists, at the home of a prominent woman of high society. Her mother's salon at the Hermitage had been well known and attended by high-ranking Americans and British leaders. During the American Revolution and before her marriage, patriots, Loyalists, and commanders from both sides of the war had attended her mother's salon. George Washington, Nathanael Greene, Henry Knox, Alexander Hamilton (officers during the American Revolution), James Madison and James Monroe (future American presidents), and her future husband had all attended Theodosia Prévost's salon in New Jersey.

Present at Theo's Richmond Hill salon were young women friends such as Natalie. Theo did not leave behind lists of all the attendees, but her salon likely also included her father's political allies and young male suitors from the area's finest families and best colleges. Another regular at the salon gatherings was the famous American author Washington Irving.

Theodosia had known Washington Irving since her early days at Madame de Senat's school. Irving was a few months older than she was and attended the school across the street. His much older brother Peter was one of her father's friends, and the younger Irving became a regular visitor to the Burr home. According to Theodosia's biographer Charles Felton Pidgin, many of the Burr family friends thought Irving was utterly in love with Theodosia and hoped they would marry. Historians find no evidence that Theodosia and Irving shared anything more than close friendship and mutual admiration. But as two of New York City's young, dynamic generation, it's not surprising that speculation about them arose.

Theodosia's salon would have read and discussed the great works of their time, such as *The History of the Decline and Fall of the Roman Empire* by Edward Gibbon or classic works of the ancients, such as Roman poet Horace. When they weren't reading the classics,

Susanna Rowson (*in an undated miniature watercolor, right*) was a prolific English writer, educator, and actress. Her 1791 novel *Charlotte Temple* (*frontispiece of an 1814 edition, left*) was the most popular bestseller in American literature until the mid-nineteenth century. It was one of the novels that Theodosia and her contemporaries would have read.

Theodosia and her friends read novels for fun. Both women and men read this relatively new, popular, and widely available genre. Novels were the topic of social conversation and debate, so men often read popular novels to be able to discuss them in social settings. Many of the most popular authors were women.

In 1794 Susanna Rowson's *Charlotte Temple* was an immediate sensation. It told what was then a shocking story of a sixteen-year-old girl who runs away from London to New York with a handsome British officer. They do not marry, and he eventually abandons her—penniless, single, and pregnant. The novel was supposedly a thinly veiled telling of an actual event that had occurred during the American Revolution. The author was the real-life cousin of the callous officer, Captain John Montresor.

Washington Irving

Washington Irving was born in 1783, a few months before Theodosia was born, and he grew up in the same circle of friends. His mother named him after George Washington. As a boy, Irving attended a school across the street from Madame De Senat's academy, where Theodosia studied French. His older brother, Peter, was a friend and political ally of Aaron Burr.

Irving wasn't interested in school or a career in law, although he studied law and passed the New York bar exam. Instead, he enjoyed writing. His first published work was a series of letters written under the pseudonym Jonathan Oldstyle to the *Morning Chronicle* newspaper in 1802. The letters poked fun

John Wesley Jarvis painted this portrait of author Washington Irving in 1809.

at New York society. In 1807 Irving started a literary magazine called *Salmagundi* with his brother and a friend. (The word *salmagundi* comes from the French word *salmigondis* and refers to a recipe that calls for a wide mix of meats and vegetables.) Again writing under pseudonyms, Irving produced articles for the magazine that made fun of New York social life and politics.

In 1809 Irving published *A History of New-York from the Beginning of the World to the End of the Dutch Dynasty* under the name of Diedrich Knickerbocker. A satirical look at New York history and politics, it was popular both in the United States and in England. Since the publication of the book, New Yorkers have been known as Knickerbockers. The name of the New York Knicks (Knickerbockers) basketball team comes from that term.

Irving is best known for his stories "Rip Van Winkle" and "The Legend of Sleepy Hollow." Sunnyside, his home in Tarrytown, New York, is a National Historic Site and is open to the public. Learn more at https://hudsonvalley.org/historic-sites/washington-irvings-sunnyside/.

Ann Radcliffe's romantic adventure, *The Mysteries of Udolpho* (1794), transported readers to an exotic Italian castle where the main character, a teenaged girl, is held prisoner by her aunt's husband. Other romantic novels such as *Memoirs of Emma Courtney* (1796) by Mary Hays and Maria Edgeworth's *Castle Rackrent* (1800) were also on everyone's reading list.

Novels of manners instructed young women in proper virtuous behavior. *Pamela, or Virtue Rewarded* by Samuel Richardson (1740) was on every young woman's reading list for decades. Yet many women sneered at Richardson's instruction manual for the "perfect woman" as a manual that rewarded passivity and submission as the keys to social success. Writers such as Eliza Haywood, in her book *The Anti-Pamela, or Feign'd Innocence Detected* (1741) brutally mocked it by presenting the protagonist as a shameless social climber who pretends to be meek to get ahead.

Fanny Burney's 1778 novel, *Evelina, or the History of a Young Lady's Entrance into the World,* told the story of the English upper class through the eyes of a seventeen-year-old girl. It featured a woman protagonist, which was unusual for that time. It made fun of the masculine values that shaped women's lives. It also pointed out the hypocrisies of upper-class sexual attitudes, which expected women to behave publicly in a wholesome manner while being available to men for sexual pleasure.

SPECTACULAR CITY, SPECTACULAR THEODOSIA

Eventually, all the lessons in penmanship, geography, history, literature, Latin, Greek, French, music, dancing, and etiquette coalesced into a spectacular, unique young woman: Theodosia Burr. Amazingly to many, her masculine education didn't clash with her feminine qualities. Theodosia was gracious, spontaneous, and charming. And smart. Biographer Charles Felton Pidgin called her "the First Gentlewoman of Her Time." Theodosia was something that hadn't been seen before. She

> "Mr. Burr introduced me to his daughter [then fifteen] whom he has educated with uncommon care; for she is elegant without ostentation, and learned without pedantry. At the time she dances with more grace than any young lady of New York. Miss Theodosia speaks French and Italian with facility, is perfectly conversant with the writers of the Augustan age."
>
> —John Davis, English visitor to New York, 1798

was as comfortable with small talk in a general social setting as she was with scholarly discussions in a closed parlor. She moved effortlessly from one to the other. Theodosia took her mother's example and carried it to the next level, that of a fully and formally educated gentlewoman.

A sought-after member of New York City's society, she received far more invitations than she was able to accept. Her father gave her advice on how to choose which to turn down and how to say no without hurting a hostess's feelings. She learned to master her emotions and never display rudeness or dislike of someone. She easily won over skeptics of Burr's educational experiment who doubted Theodosia was entirely a woman.

By the end of the eighteenth century, New York was also coming into its own. The city had become home to twenty-two houses of worship that represented thirteen different religious denominations: Dutch Reformed, Protestant Episcopal (formerly the Church of England), French Huguenot, Quaker, Lutheran, Jewish, Presbyterian, Baptist, Moravian, German Reformed, Methodist, Roman Catholic, and Independent Congregational. Theodosia often attended the Sunday morning Roman Catholic services with Madame de Senat and Natalie. And by then, Trinity Church had been rebuilt at its original site on Broadway. Its towering steeple marked the beginning of Wall Street, which ran downhill to the East River.

The thriving city offered countless possibilities for new experiences and entertainment. The nation's political capital had moved to Philadelphia, but New York remained the financial and social capital of the new nation. Always an international city, the growing metropolis had many different cultures contributing to it. Without ever having to leave the island, Theodosia would have encountered and known people from Dutch, Irish, Scottish, English, Austrian, German, French, Italian, Spanish, Portuguese, African, and Middle Eastern backgrounds.

Newspapers reported on happenings around the United States and the rest of the world. New Yorkers gathered in taverns and coffeehouses to discuss the latest financial and scientific advancements. Booksellers stocked the most recent novels, musical scores, and books of all kinds. Shops sold exotic foods, spices, fabrics, and teas. New Yorkers always debated politics, and Theodosia's father was often the topic of conversation. Burr was distinguishing himself as an up-and-coming leader of New York's Democratic-Republicans, who supported Thomas Jefferson's political philosophy, which included more power for the states and independent banking rather than a central government bank. Heading the opposing party, the Federalists, was Alexander Hamilton. The two parties would become rivals in just a few years, leading to bitter personal animosity between Hamilton and Burr.

The best musicians and actors of their time, on tour in New York from England and Europe, performed the latest music, dance, and theater. Theodosia and Natalie often caused a sensation when they attended. Everyone was anxious to speak to the intriguing Miss Burr to see what she was really like. They were not disappointed. Even the brightest young men were unable to find a question she couldn't politely answer. Washington Irving said Theodosia gracefully bettered them all!

As Theodosia walked along the cobblestones of Wall Street, she passed the city's new icons of progress. These buildings included Pierre L'Enfant's Federal Hall, the Manhattan Company (of which her father was a founder), Alexander Hamilton's Bank of New York, and the

Francis Guy painted this view of the Tontine Coffeehouse, which once stood at the corner of Wall and Water Streets in New York City, in 1797. It was a popular gathering place for Wall Street financiers. The painting is occasionally on view as part of the New-York Historical Society's collection.

United States Bank. The city's financiers socialized at the Merchants and Tontine coffeehouses. Traders with the New York Stock Exchange bought and sold stock in new and growing companies, meeting right out in the open on the street. Wherever Theodosia went, she was greeted with "Good afternoon, Miss Burr," and a polite bow.

At night the town's families socialized at dinner parties, discussing some of the most innovative ideas about commerce and science. In just a few years, Robert Fulton would build his famous steamship, and Governor DeWitt Clinton would approve the building of the Erie Canal to link the Great Lakes to the Atlantic Ocean via the Hudson River. Elegant balls were held for special occasions. Theodosia was accustomed to meeting and socializing with a generation of Americans who would one day become household names and find a place in history books. The most eligible men of the city sought after her companionship.

8

Theodosia Burr Alston

In the end, it was Theodosia, not her father, who chose Joseph Alston as her husband.

—*Richard N. Côté, Theodosia Burr biographer*

Theodosia was a vibrant, intelligent, and stunning young woman. Petite, with long, dark auburn hair and her father's dark eyes, she had many admirers. One afternoon, when Theodosia was sixteen, she took a walk with New York's mayor Edward Livingston. Together, they toured a French warship visiting the city. Remarking on her lively personality, Livingston jovially warned her, "Now, Theodosia, you must bring none of your sparks on board. They have a [gunpowder barrel], and we should all be blown up!"

But not everyone was prepared for a young lady as unusual as Miss Theodosia Burr. Robert Troup, who was Alexander Hamilton's roommate at King's College and a friend of Theodosia's father, remarked that "her acquaintance say her reading has been wholly masculine, that she is an utter stranger to the use of the needle, and quite unskilled in the different branches of domestic economy." He

John Vanderlyn painted Theodosia's official wedding portrait in 1800, the year before her marriage. The artist told her father, whose portrait he also painted, that the painting of Theodosia was the best portrait he ever painted in the United States. It hangs in the main gallery of the New-York Historical Society. Her honeymoon visit to Niagara Falls popularized the site as a honeymoon destination.

meant that she did not have the typical education viewed as suitable for a wife and mother at that time.

In 1798, one year after finishing his term in the US Senate, Aaron Burr was elected again to the New York Assembly, by then in Albany, the state capital. Theodosia accompanied her father while he served his term. She returned to the city of her birth as a phenomenon and celebrity. Theodosia was at her father's side in 1799 when the battle he started in 1784 over the abolition of slavery in the state of New York was won. Governor John Jay signed the bill into law.

The following year, in August 1800, Theodosia joined her father on the campaign trail supporting the election of Thomas Jefferson for president and Burr for vice president. The presidential election between incumbent John Adams and his challenger, Vice President Thomas Jefferson, was coming up. "The country is beautiful, some of the views are really charming and the inhabitants are hospitable,"

Theodosia wrote to her half brother John Bartow. Burr, a master political strategist, went to Providence, Rhode Island, to campaign for Jefferson (and for himself) and to ensure local support for the two candidates. Joseph Alston, a young man from South Carolina and one of Burr's acquaintances, was sightseeing in the Northeast and was also on the same trip. When Alston returned to South Carolina, he wrote to Theodosia professing his love for her. In December she invited him to visit her in New York.

THE RICE PLANTER

Joseph Alston was born in 1779 in All Saints Parish near Georgetown, South Carolina. He was four years older than Theodosia and had attended the College of New Jersey (Princeton). Alston studied law under Edward Rutledge (one of the youngest signers of the Declaration of Independence) and passed the South Carolina bar exam in 1799.

He decided the practice of law wasn't for him and chose to become a plantation owner instead. Eventually, he owned about 6,287 acres (2,544 ha) of land and was one of the wealthiest men of the South Carolina aristocracy.

An unidentified artist made this portrait of Joseph Alston. It is one of only two known surviving images of him.

Presidential Election of 1800

In 1800 the nation's fourth presidential election pitted incumbent John Adams, a Federalist from Massachusetts, against his vice president, Thomas Jefferson, a Democratic-Republican from Virginia. At that time, voters didn't elect presidents. Electors, chosen by the state legislatures, elected them. Candidates ran as individuals rather than on a combined presidential–vice presidential ticket as in modern elections. The person with the most votes became president, and the candidate with the second most votes became vice president.

The campaigns were filled with harsh debate between the two political parties and among the regions of the country they represented. Former treasury secretary Alexander Hamilton led the Federalists, who were mostly northerners. They advocated for more federal control over the states and a closer political alignment with Great Britain. Thomas Jefferson led the Democratic-Republicans, who were mostly southerners. They argued for less federal authority and more state sovereignty (the right of states to run their own governments without interference from a central government). New York, in the middle geographically and divided politically between both parties, became the pivotal swing state in the election.

Alexander Hamilton disliked John Adams. He believed Adams was unqualified to remain in office and wrote a scathing pamphlet that ridiculed his presidency. This caused a scandal that led to losses for the Federalists in New York. Aaron Burr, running to be Thomas Jefferson's vice president, successfully led New York's Democratic-Republicans to victory. When the states cast their electoral votes, they unexpectedly split them evenly between Jefferson and Burr. They tied with seventy-three each. Adams won sixty-five electoral votes, while his vice presidential running mate Charles Pinckney of South Carolina won sixty-four.

According to the US Constitution, choosing the president became the duty of the House of Representatives when electoral votes were tied. Voting thirty-five times, representatives were unable to choose between Jefferson and Burr. Alexander Hamilton, still irritated at Burr's success in delivering New York's votes for Democratic-Republicans, convinced some New York representatives to switch their votes. On the thirty-sixth round of voting, on February 17, 1801, representatives chose Jefferson for president and Burr as vice president.

Theodosia Burr Alston

Most young women would have been ecstatic to receive attention from a man of Alston's social status. But Theodosia was no average young woman. She was the embodiment of Mary Wollstonecraft's philosophy, an intelligent, educated, independent, and capable woman. Alston was the product of Chesterfield's view of women as children and men as their caretakers and masters in life. How would Theodosia receive his advances? How would Alston react to her assertiveness? And how would Theodosia, raised in an environment opposed to slavery, fit into a plantation culture with more than two hundred slaves?

New Yorkers gossiped about their relationship. Many considered southerners slow and backward. South Carolina was nothing but a backwoods swamp, they declared. Why would Theodosia Burr ever consider going there? And after a lifetime among New York's most talented young men, why pick a rice planter? Some even proposed that her father, who was in debt, had arranged for a marriage to the wealthy man, in the hopes that Alston would cover those debts. Parents often chose their children's spouses to enhance the family's property holdings or monetary wealth or to move up on the social ladder. After meeting Alston, some New Yorkers proclaimed that he was slow-witted and unattractive, far beneath what Theodosia Burr deserved.

But the December visit was a success, and afterward, Alston wrote her a marriage proposal. She accepted. But she wrote to Alston that like the ancient Greek philosopher Aristotle, she was opposed to early marriage. Theodosia tested Alston, saying to him that "Aristotle says that a man should not marry before he is six-and-thirty; pray, Mr. Alston, what arguments have you to oppose such authority?"

Alston took on the challenge. He wrote a lengthy response in support of not delaying marriage.

"Hear me, Miss Burr. It has always been my practice, whether from a natural independence of mind, from pride, or what other cause I will not pretend to say, never to adopt the opinion of anyone, however respectable his authority, unless thoroughly convinced by his arguments . . . even of Cicero [an ancient Roman philosopher and statesman] who stands higher in my estimation than any other author . . . therefore, till you offer better reasons in support of his opinion than the Grecian sage himself [Aristotle] has done, excuse my differing from him."

The letter went on for many pages. In it, Alston tells of his childhood and education, admission to the bar, business success, and travels to prove to Theodosia that he was mature enough to marry. But he didn't stop there. He launched into a full explanation and defense of life in South Carolina. The city of Charleston, he said, is "the most delightfully situated city in America . . . cooled by the refreshing seabreeze." He pointed out that, contrary to the beliefs of New Yorkers, South Carolinians were not boorish or rude or uncultured. He wrote that the women "are perfectly easy and agreeable in their manners and remarkably fond of company; no Charleston belle [pretty young lady] ever felt any ennui [boredom] in her life." Touché.

Alston's romantic portrait of South Carolina was one that even many South Carolinians disagreed with. The plantations were, in fact, sweltering, mosquito-infested lands that bred sicknesses such as yellow fever and malaria. The wives and daughters of plantation owners complained of constant boredom and isolation. Jane Lynch, the mistress of Greenfield Plantation on the Black River in Georgetown County, complained about the "everlasting routine of plantation life." Most striking about Alston's letter is the complete lack of discussion of slavery, something Theodosia Burr would have to come to terms with if she agreed to marry him.

She didn't seem to mind Alston's contradictions. She had found her match, and she was madly in love.

On February 2, 1801, Theodosia Burr became Theodosia Burr Alston in a ceremony in Albany. The couple was married in a church service and spent one week there. Then they traveled to the South, where they met with her father in Baltimore, Maryland. The Alstons accompanied him to Washington, DC, where, on March 4, Thomas Jefferson was sworn in as the third president of the United States, with Aaron Burr as his vice president.

Theodosia Burr Alston, with the husband she had chosen for herself at her side, watched as her father took the oath of office. He had reached the height of his political career, and she was proud of her father's achievement. She had no way of knowing the tragedies that lay ahead.

A SOUTHERN BELLE?

The Alstons' honeymoon trip took them through Upstate New York, to Niagara Falls, and into Canada to visit Theo's old friend Chief Joseph Brant. After the trip, they settled in at the Oaks, the Alston estate in South Carolina, where Theodosia became mistress of the massive plantation there. She was welcomed by the Alston family and the southern society ladies. She continued writing regularly to her father and brothers and they to her.

As warmly as Theodosia was welcomed into South Carolina society, nothing prepared her for the difference between life on a plantation and life at Richmond Hill in New York. When she and Alston arrived, the family and their two hundred slaves gathered to greet the newlyweds, as was customary. The mistress of a plantation was expected to handle all matters concerning the well-being of the plantation's slaves, including housing, food, and medical care. Theodosia never wrote about her feelings or attitudes about slavery. New Yorkers accepted southern slavery as fact, even if they did not agree with it. Americans had spoken out against slavery as early as the late seventeenth century. But the United States didn't officially abolish slavery until the passage of the Thirteenth Amendment to the US Constitution in 1865.

Accustomed to the active society of New York, Theodosia Burr Alston found herself isolated. Her nearest neighbors were on

This undated landscape painting of a southern plantation dates to about 1825. The artist's technique is similar to the stitches of embroidery, which girls from well-to-do homes of the time would have mastered as part of their education.

plantations miles away. When she had an opportunity to socialize, she found that South Carolina culture was no match for the intellectual stimulation she had grown up with. Instead, the Chesterfieldian rules her parents had rebelled against dominated it.

While Theodosia was adjusting to married life, her childhood companion Natalie de l'Age embarked on her own adventure. Her mother had returned to France (the French Revolution was over), and de l'Age longed to see her. Burr agreed and financed her trip to France. He arranged for her to travel with Thomas Sumter Jr., whose father had been a general in the American Revolution. Sumter was on his way to Paris to serve on the staff of the American ambassador to France, Robert Livingston. During the journey, de l'Age and Sumter fell in love, and they married in Paris with her mother's approval. The Sumters settled in South Carolina.

MOTHERHOOD

On about May 22, 1802, Aaron Burr Alston was born. (Historical records aren't clear about his birthdate.) He was Theodosia's only child. When he was three weeks old, she traveled with him to New York, where she stayed for the next few months. This was her means of escape from the stifling summer heat and equally stifling social world of South Carolina. She spent five to six months every year with her son at Richmond Hill, with or without her husband. This was shockingly independent for a woman of that time. But Theodosia had been raised to be exactly that: self-confident in her thoughts and actions.

Alston visited New York when he could. He had been elected to the South Carolina legislature and had business there. Theodosia wrote to him lovingly during their separations. "Ah, my husband, why are we separated? Even my amusements serve to increase my unhappiness; for if any thing affords me pleasure, the thought that, were you here, you also would feel pleasure, and thus redouble [increase] mine."

Theodosia continued to support her father's political career and to join him whenever possible. In 1804, Burr ran for governor of New York against New York lawyer and politician Morgan Lewis. The New York newspapers were filled

This unattributed oil painting of Theodosia was made in 1802 or 1803 at about the time her son was born. It is part of the Yale University art gallery collection.

with vicious stories about Burr. One of the stories included a letter from Charles D. Cooper, a young man who had attended a dinner party with Alexander Hamilton. In it, he enumerated a list of insults Hamilton had made at the party about Burr. Hamilton's role in the 1800 presidential election, in which he had taken steps to make sure Burr became vice president rather than president, was still festering in the minds of Burr and many New Yorkers. Burr wrote to Hamilton and asked him to disavow the comments Cooper had shared. A series of letters passed between the two enemies throughout the spring. Dissatisfied and disappointed, Burr challenged Hamilton to a duel. Hamilton accepted.

THE DUEL

Before the duel, Burr wrote his will in case he died in the challenge. He also wrote a letter to Theodosia in which he explained his wishes. He told her that she and her husband were to be joint executors of his estate. (Executors make financial, legal, and other decisions for a person after they are dead.) Burr requested that his servant Peggy Garten receive a parcel of his land and a cash bonus for her service. He left instructions for the handling of his personal papers and correspondence and requested that Natalie Sumter receive one of his portraits. He closed with a declaration of his love for his daughter. "I am indebted to you, my dearest Theodosia, for a very great portion of the happiness which I have enjoyed in this life. You have completely satisfied all that my heart and affections had hoped or even wished."

The duel between Burr and Hamilton took place on July 11, 1804, in Weehawken, New Jersey, across the Hudson River from New York City. Burr shot Hamilton, who died the following day. New York outlawed dueling, but New Jersey hadn't. The encounter followed that state's rules of dueling, so Burr was not tried for murder. But many people viewed Burr as a murderer, and the slander followed him for the rest of his life. He never recovered his political reputation.

Dueling

Dueling is a type of prearranged combat between two people, using the same type of weapon. A code duello, or code of dueling, established the strict rules and proper procedures for conducting a duel. The rules differed by region. In the United States in the eighteenth century, the weapon of choice was the pistol. Then politeness and manners played a large and important role in daily life. Outward displays of anger or aggression were frowned upon, as was public insult. A violation of these social rules was considered an insult to a person's honor and often ended in a duel. Dueling was so common during this time that gentlemen often had a set of dueling pistols.

In 1804 James Cheetham, editor of the *New York American Citizen* newspaper, accused his rival editor, William Coleman of the *New York Evening Post,* of fathering a biracial child out of wedlock. Interracial relationships were extremely controversial, as well as illegal. So Coleman, known to be skilled with a pistol, challenged Cheetham to a duel. But Judge Henry Brockholst Livingston ordered them both arrested. Livingston had killed a man in a duel a few years before and had regretted it. He opposed dueling and refused to release Coleman and Cheetham from jail unless they swore an oath, as gentlemen, not to duel. Later, Jeremiah Thompson, a friend of Cheetham, accused Coleman of cowardice. So Coleman challenged Thompson to a duel and killed him. The duel was north of New York City on a rural path, Love Lane, at what is now Twenty-First Street between Sixth Avenue and Eighth Avenue.

Later that year, Aaron Burr killed former treasury secretary Alexander Hamilton in a duel. Three years earlier, in 1801, New York lawyer George Eacker had killed Hamilton's oldest son Philip—who was only nineteen years old—in a duel. Although the men involved in these two duels lived in New York, the duels were held in New Jersey. To reduce the number of duels, New York had outlawed the practice. By the late nineteenth century, dueling had become unpopular and faded out.

This undated illustration from the nineteenth century depicts the famous duel in 1804 in which Burr shot and killed Hamilton. The men's seconds (backups) stand behind a nearby tree.

Burr's reputation also suffered from an ill-considered plan to create a different country west of the Mississippi River. After he had finished his term as vice president, Burr journeyed to the Ohio River valley, then part of the western frontier. There, he leased 40,000 acres (16,190 ha) of land stretching from Pittsburgh, Pennsylvania, to Wheeling, Virginia. (West Virginia was not yet a state. The acreage that interested Burr was part of land that belonged to Spain, so Burr leased it from Spain.) When President Jefferson heard that Burr was planning to use that land to start a separate country, Burr was arrested and tried in 1807 for treason.

Theodosia accompanied her father to the trial in Richmond, Virginia. Burr was found not guilty. Due to the disgrace of the duel and the trial, Burr left the United States and spent the next four years traveling throughout Europe. In 1809, when she was twenty-six, Theodosia wrote to her friend Dolley Madison, then the First Lady, the wife of President James Madison. (Burr had played matchmaker during his Senate term, introducing the two. The Madisons

Theodosia Burr Alston

Beyond Theodosia

Aaron Burr was a very visible, public person. He was also intensely private. Mystery still surrounds some aspects of his private life, and historians are unsure whether he had children with women other than his wife.

The most sensational of those rumors is that Burr was the biological father of Martin Van Buren (1782–1862), the eighth president of the United States. Van Buren was born in Kinderhook, New York, not far from Albany, six months before the birth of Burr's daughter Theodosia. Burr had legal business in Kinderhook, and locals claimed he had had an affair with a Maria Van Buren. The question of Burr's parentage of Van Buren is one of the main themes in Gore Vidal's book *Burr*, a fictional biography of Burr, published in 1973.

Oral stories suggest that Burr fathered two children—a girl, Louisa Charlotte Burr, and a boy, John Pierre Burr—with an East Indian servant while he was a senator in Philadelphia. The woman may have been named Mary Emmons or Eugénie Beauharnais (historians aren't sure), and she had been brought to Philadelphia from Haiti. Burr wrote openly to his male friends about his affairs with women (and later to Theodosia when she was an adult about his affairs in France). Yet no woman by either of these names or descriptions appears in any of his letters.

Rumors of other Burr children continued into the nineteenth century. Historians are unsure if the stories are based on solid evidence or if they were rumors started by his political enemies to harm his reputation.

maintained a friendship with the Burrs after that.) Theodosia hoped that Dolley Madison would be able to intercede on her father's behalf so that he would be able to return home. Many people still believed Burr was guilty of treason even though he had not been convicted. A statement from the president reaffirming his innocence would clear his name and allow Burr to regain his reputation. Dolley Madison wrote back to Theodosia that although she had great affection for her, her husband, the president, declined to act in Burr's favor. Three years later, in 1812, Burr returned to New York and eventually resumed his law practice.

HEARTBROKEN

The Alstons' ten-year-old son, Aaron, died on June 30, 1812, most likely from malaria. Theodosia wrote an anguished letter to her father in New York. "There is no more joy for me. The world is a blank. I have lost my boy. My child is gone for ever." She sank into a deep depression.

A few months later, on December 10, 1812, Joseph Alston became the forty-fourth governor of South Carolina. Alston, worried about his wife's health and state of mind, wrote to his father-in-law. Together, they decided she should travel to New York. They hoped the companionship there and a return to her home would help her to recover from the depression that gripped her.

She agreed, and on December 31, 1812, she boarded the schooner (a small sailing ship) *Patriot* for the trip northward along the Atlantic coast from South Carolina to New York. She brought with her a few trunks, in which she placed all of her father's personal papers as well as much of her own personal correspondence. The ship never arrived in New York, and she, the other passengers, and the crew were never seen again. No one ever found the body of the schooner nor the trunks containing the Burr family papers, which Burr had been planning to use to write a memoir. Both husband and father were inconsolable. Burr confided to a friend, "When I realized the truth of her death, the world became a blank to me, and life had then lost all its value." And to his son-in-law, he wrote that with the loss of his beloved daughter, he was "severed from the human race."

Alston never recovered from the loss of his son and wife. After his term as governor, he became ill and died in 1815. He was thirty-six years old.

9

What Happened to Theodosia?

No father ever more loved a child, nor more laboriously proved his love, than Aaron Burr. No child ever repaid a father's care and tenderness, with a love more constant and devoted than Theodosia.
—James Parton, Aaron Burr biographer, 1858

Theodosia's sudden and mysterious disappearance spawned many theories and speculative novels about what happened to her. One of the most accepted was that the ship went down at sea during a hurricane. Another more lurid explanation was that pirates captured the ship. Pirate vessels sometimes roamed the Atlantic coast, looking for ships to rob. Alston and Burr preferred to believe the hurricane story rather than the gruesome and terrifying pirate theory. But as time went on, the pirate theories grew, spread, and gave rise to speculations about her fate. Burr rejected them all.

Modern historians are divided on Theodosia Burr Alston's fate. The lack of solid evidence makes it difficult to determine exactly what happened to the *Patriot*. Years later, on his deathbed, a man confessed

Leslie Odom Jr. played Aaron Burr in the Broadway hit musical *Hamilton*, written by Lin-Manuel Miranda. Odom won the 2016 Tony Award for Best Actor in a Musical for his performance and the Grammy Award for Best Musical Theater Album as a principal vocalist.

to having been one of the pirates who boarded the ship and said that she had been forced overboard to drown in the sea. But some historians doubt the man was referring to the *Patriot*. The lack of survivors and the missing ship make it impossible to determine what occurred.

Theodosia's life was short. She presumably died just shy of her thirtieth birthday, yet her accomplishments lived on and inspired the next generations of American women. Burr's model of the new American woman—educated, capable, and independent—began to take hold. American women were pushing for gender-based equality in the law, education, and home life, and in 1837, Oberlin College in Ohio became the first college to admit women.

The father-daughter relationship gained prominence in Lin-Manuel Miranda's megahit musical *Hamilton*. It premiered in New York on Broadway in 2015, and it continues to tour across the country. In the musical, the character of Aaron Burr sings about his love for his newborn daughter and the hopes he has for her great future. Little did he know that he and Theodosia were setting the stage for a time when fathers would routinely mentor their daughters, participate in their education, and encourage them to achieve their dreams. Aaron Burr and Theodosia Burr Alston live on in many father-daughter relationships of the twenty-first century.

Timeline

1746	Theodosia Bartow is born in New Jersey.
1756	Aaron Burr is born in New Jersey.
1769	Aaron Burr enters Princeton College.
1772	Aaron Burr graduates from Princeton College.
1775	The American Revolution begins, and Aaron Burr enlists in the Continental Army. He serves until the war ends.
1782	Aaron Burr and Theodosia Bartow Prévost are married.
1783	Theodosia Burr is born in June in Albany, New York.
1784	Theodosia and her family move to New York City.
1789	George Washington is inaugurated as the first president of the United States.
1790s	Natalie de l'Age de Volude and Madame de Senat and her daughter arrive in New York City as refugees from the French Revolution.
1794	Theodosia's mother, Theodosia Bartow Prévost Burr, dies.
1797	Theodosia holds a state dinner for Chief Joseph Brant, the Mohawk chief of the Six Iroquois Nations.
1800	Theodosia is introduced to Joseph Alston while on a campaign trip through New England with her father.
1801	Theodosia Burr and Joseph Alston marry in Albany, New York.
1802	Aaron Burr Alston is born in South Carolina.
1812	Aaron Burr Alston dies.
	Theodosia Burr Alston boards a ship, the *Patriot*, to travel from South Carolina to New York. The ship and its passengers are all lost at sea.
1815	Joseph Alston dies in South Carolina.
1836	Aaron Burr dies in Staten Island, New York.